An Analysis of Data on Rape and Sexual Assault

Sex Offenses and Offenders

About 234,000 convicted sex offenders are under the care, custody, or control of corrections agencies on an average day. Nearly 60% are under conditional supervision in the community.

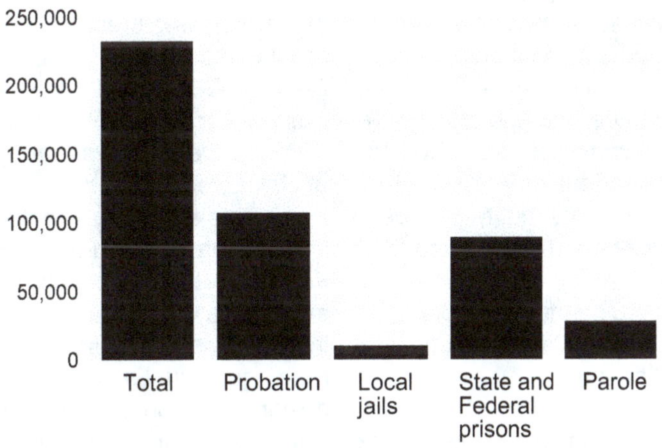

250,000	
200,000	
150,000	
100,000	
50,000	
0	Total Probation Local jails State and Federal prisons Parole

Foreword

This report draws on more than two dozen statistical datasets maintained by the Bureau of Justice Statistics and the Uniform Crime Reporting program of the FBI to provide a comprehensive overview of current knowledge about the incidence and prevalence of violent victimization by sexual assault, the response of the justice system to such crimes, and the characteristics of those who prey on victims of all ages by committing sexual assault or rape.

This report reinforces a striking observation in recent studies about crimes involving rape and sexual assault: In a high percentage of cases, the victims are children. In self-reported victimization surveys of the public age 12 and older, teenagers report the highest per capita rates of exposure to rape and sexual assault. Data drawn from police-recorded incidents of rape in three States revealed that 44% of rape victims were under the age of 18. The self-reports of convicted rape and sexual assault offenders serving time in State prisons indicate that two-thirds of such offenders had victims under the age of 18, and 58% of those — or nearly 4 in 10 imprisoned violent sex offenders — said their victims were age 12 or younger.

Though the vast majority of violent sex offending involves males assaulting female victims, females account for a small percentage of known offenders, and males account for a small percentage of victims. In a very small fraction of sexual assaults, victim and offender are of the same sex.

Victim and offender are likely to have had a prior relationship as family members, intimates, or acquaintances. Victims of rape and sexual assault report that in nearly 3 out of 4 incidents, the offender was not a stranger. Based on police-recorded incident data, in 90% of the rapes of children younger than 12, the child knew the offender; two-thirds of the victims 18 to 29 years old had a prior relationship with the rapist. The FBI's UCR arrest data, as well as court conviction data and prison admissions data, all point to a sex offender who is older than other violent offenders, generally in his early thirties, and more likely to be white than other violent offenders — characteristics that match the information obtained from victims who describe the offender to interviewers in the National Crime Victimization Survey.

This report was prepared as background information for the Assistant Attorney General's 1996 National Summit *Promoting Public Safety Through the Effective Management of Sex Offenders in the Community*. It presents a thorough analysis and compilation of the currently available national data, but we anticipate that even more will be learned in the coming years as BJS assembles data on rape and sexual assault from the redesigned National Crime Victimization Survey and surveys of felony probationers, local jail inmates, and State and Federal prison inmates.

Jan M. Chaiken, Ph.D.
Director, Bureau of Justice Statistics

Laurie Robinson
Assistant Attorney General
Office of Justice Programs

Highlights

Measuring the extent of sex offending

The reports from victims

In 1995 persons age 12 or older reported experiencing an estimated 260,300 attempted or completed rapes and nearly 95,000 threatened or completed sexual assaults other than rape.

- The number reported by victims age 12 or older in 1995 declined significantly from 1993:
    - 1993 — 1 violent sex offense for every 435 residents
    - 1995 — 1 violent sex offense for every 625 residents.

- In 1994 and 1995 a third of the victims said that the rape/sexual assault victimization was reported to a law enforcement agency.

The law enforcement response

In 1995 the number of forcible rapes reported to the police nationwide was 97,460, the lowest total since 1989.

- The highest rate of forcible rape recorded by law enforcement agencies since 1976 was in 1992 — 84 per 100,000 women, or about 1 forcible rape for every 1,200 women. By 1995 the rate had decreased over 14%.

- In 1995 law enforcement agencies reported that about half of all reported forcible rapes were cleared by an arrest — an estimated 34,650 arrests for forcible rape. There were 94,500 arrests for other sex offenses.

The per capita rate of arrest for forcible rape or sexual assault in 1995, 50.3 per 100,000 residents, was the same as that in 1983.

Federal statistical series obtaining data on arrested or convicted persons — Uniform Crime Reports, National Judicial Reporting Program, and National Corrections Reporting Program — show a remarkable similarity in the characteristics of those categorized as rapists: 99 in 100 are male, 6 in 10 are white, and the average age is the early thirties.

Pretrial release and adjudication of rape offenders

About half of rape defendants are released prior to trial. Among those released, half had to post a financial bond. The median bond amount was $23,500.

- About 1 in 20 filings for a violent felony in the 75 largest counties in 1992 were for rape.

- In 1992 an estimated 21,655 felony defendants nationwide were convicted of rape; 8 in 10 had pleaded guilty.

- Over two-thirds of convicted rape defendants received a prison sentence.

- For rape defendants sentenced to prison, the average term imposed was just under 14 years. About 2% of convicted rapists received life sentences.

Corrections and the convicted sex offender

On a given day about 234,000 offenders convicted of rape or sexual assault are under the care, custody, or control of corrections agencies. About 60% of these sex offenders are under conditional supervision in the community.

Rape and sexual assault offenders account for just under 5% of the total correctional population in the United States:

• Among 906,000 offenders confined in State prisons in 1994, 88,000, or 9.7%, were violent sex offenders.

• Since 1980 the average annual growth in the number of prisoners has been about 7.6%. The number of prisoners sentenced for violent sexual assault other than rape increased by an annual average of nearly 15% — faster than any other category of violent crime and faster than all other categories except drug trafficking.

• While the average sentence of convicted rapists released from State prisons has remained stable at about 10 years, the average time served has increased from about 3½ years to about 5 years; for those released after serving time for sexual assault, the sentence has been a stable 6½ years, and the average time served grew about 6 months to just under 3 years.

• Rapists and sexual assaulters serving time in State prisons were less likely to have had a prior conviction history or a history of violence than other incarcerated violent offenders, though they were substantially more likely to have had a history of convictions for violent sex offenses.

• Sexual assault offenders were substantially more likely than any other category of offenders to report having experienced physical or sexual abuse while growing up.

• Violent sex offenders were substantially less likely than other violent offenders to have committed their crime with a weapon; however, rapists were about as likely as all violent offenders to report having used a knife.

• In two 3-year BJS followups of samples of felons placed on probation and of felons released from prison, rapists had a lower rate of rearrest for a new violent felony than most other categories of offenders convicted of violence. Yet, rapists were more likely than others to be re-arrested for a new rape.

Sex offenses and murder

After the latter half of the 1980's, the percentage of all murders with known circumstances in which investigators identified rape or another sex offense as the principal circumstance of the murder has declined from about 2% of murders to less than 1%.

• Between 1976 and 1994 there were an estimated 405,089 murders in the United States. Of these, the circumstances surrounding the murder are known in 317,925, or 78.5%. Among the cases with known circumstances, an estimated 4,807, or 1.5%, were classified as involving rape or another sex offense.

• Offenders in sexual assault murders are about 6 years younger on average than other murderers. Youth under 18 have accounted for about 10% of the sexual assault murders since 1976.

How the extent of sex offending is measured

Preliminary estimates for 1995 indicate that the public age 12 or older experienced 260,300 rapes and attempted rapes and nearly 95,000 other sexual assaults and threats of sexual assault.[1]

The National Crime Victimization Survey (NCVS) is one of two statistical series maintained by the Department of Justice to learn about the incidence and prevalence of crime. The NCVS, begun in 1972, was designed to complement what is known about crimes reported to local law enforcement agencies under the FBI's annual compilation known as the Uniform Crime Reports (UCR).

The NCVS gathers information about crime and its consequences from a nationally representative sample of U.S. residents age 12 or older about any crimes they may have experienced — whether or not the crime was reported to a law enforcement agency.

[1]In the National Crime Victimization Survey, rape is defined as forced sexual intercourse where the victim may be either male or female and the offender may be of the same sex or a different sex from the victim. Sexual assault includes a wide range of victimizations involving attacks in which unwanted sexual contact occurs between the victim and the offender. Threats and attempts to commit such offenses are included in the counts.

The national sample of households, 50,000 households and more than 100,000 individual respondents, is the second largest ongoing household survey sponsored by the Federal Government.

In the latter half of the 1980's, the Bureau of Justice Statistics (BJS), together with the Committee on Law and Justice of the American Statistical Association, sought to improve the survey components to enhance the measurement of rape, sexual assault, and domestic violence. The new NCVS questions broadened the scope of covered sexual incidents beyond the categories of rape and attempted rape to include sexual assaults and other unwanted sexual contacts.

The new questions and revised procedures were phased in from January 1992 through June 1993 in half the sampled households. Since July 1993, the redesigned methods have been used for the entire national sample. Based upon the half-sample, BJS was able to determine that the new questionnaire would produce estimated rates of rape and sexual assault that were about 4 times higher than previously measured.

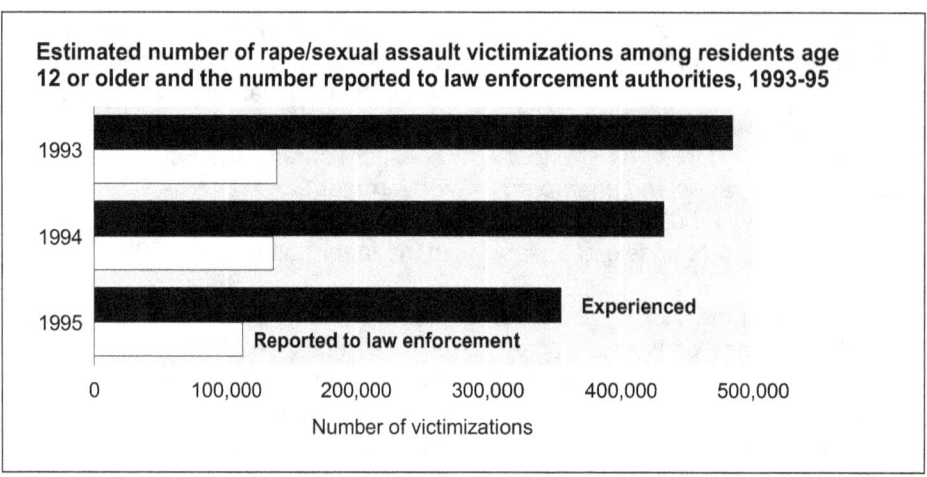

Estimated number of rape/sexual assault victimizations among residents age 12 or older and the number reported to law enforcement authorities, 1993-95

1993

1994

1995   **Experienced**

Reported to law enforcement

0   100,000   200,000   300,000   400,000   500,000

Number of victimizations

Figure 1

• The nearly 355,000 rapes and sexual assaults reported by victims in the preliminary estimates for 1995 were significantly below the number of such offenses estimated for 1993 (figure 1). In a comparison of the two years, the number of offenses experienced by victims is estimated to have dropped by a quarter and the per capita rate of rape and sexual assault to have dropped 30%. The 1993 rate translates into about 1 rape/sexual assault victimization for every 435 persons age 12 or older, and the 1995 preliminary rate equals 1 offense for every 625 residents at least 12 years old.

• For both 1994 and 1995 the percentage of rape/sexual assault victimizations reported to a law enforcement agency was 32%. The most common reason given by victims of rape/sexual assault for reporting the crime to the police was to prevent further crimes by the offender against them. The most common reason cited by the victim for not reporting the crime to the police was that it was considered a personal matter .

• In 1994 victims reported about 1 rape/sexual assault victimization of a female victim for every 270 females in the general population; for males, the rate was substantially lower, with about 1 rape/sexual assault of a male victim for every 5,000 male residents age 12 or older.

• Per capita rates of rape/sexual assault were found to be highest among residents age 16 to 19, low-income residents, and urban residents. There were no significant differences in the rate of rape/sexual assault among racial groups.

• Overall, an estimated 91% of the victims of rape and sexual assault were female. Nearly 99% of the offenders they described in single-victim incidents were male.

Characteristics of rape/sexual assault incidents

▸About two-thirds of rapes/sexual assaults were found to occur during the 12 hours from 6 p.m. to 6 a.m. (figure 2).

▸Nearly 6 out of 10 rape/sexual assault incidents were reported by victims to have occurred in their own home or at the home of a friend, relative, or neighbor (figure 3).

▸More than half of rape/sexual assault incidents were reported by victims to have occurred within 1 mile of their home or at their home.

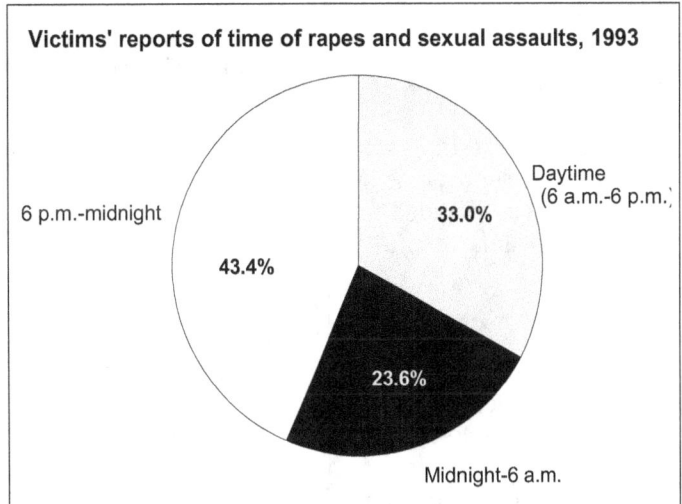

Victims' reports of time of rapes and sexual assaults, 1993

6 p.m.-midnight 43.4%

Daytime (6 a.m.-6 p.m.) 33.0%

23.6%

Midnight-6 a.m.

Figure 2

▸About 1 of every 16 rape/sexual assault victims reported that a firearm was present during the commission of the offense. Most victims (84%), however, reported that no weapon was used by the offender.

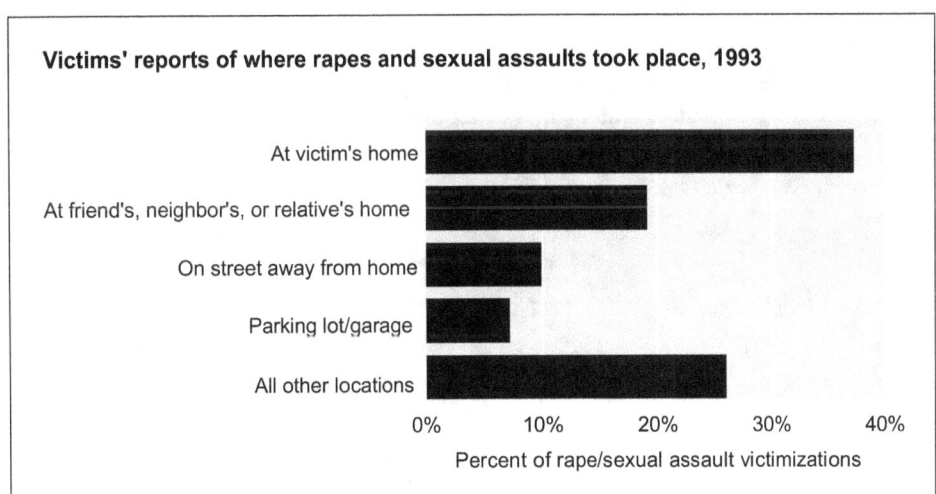

Victims' reports of where rapes and sexual assaults took place, 1993

At victim's home

At friend's, neighbor's, or relative's home

On street away from home

Parking lot/garage

All other locations

0%   10%   20%   30%   40%

Percent of rape/sexual assault victimizations

Figure 3

Characteristics of rape/sexual assault offenders as described by victims

‣About 9 out of 10 rape/sexual assault victimizations involved a single offender, according to victims' reports (figure 4).

‣Three out of four rape/sexual assault victimizations involved offenders (both single- and multiple-offender incidents) with whom the victim had a prior relationship as a family member, intimate, or acquaintance. Strangers accounted for nearly 20% of the victimizations involving a single offender but 76% of the victimizations involving multiple offenders. About 7% of all rape/sexual assault victimizations involved multiple offenders who were strangers to the victim.

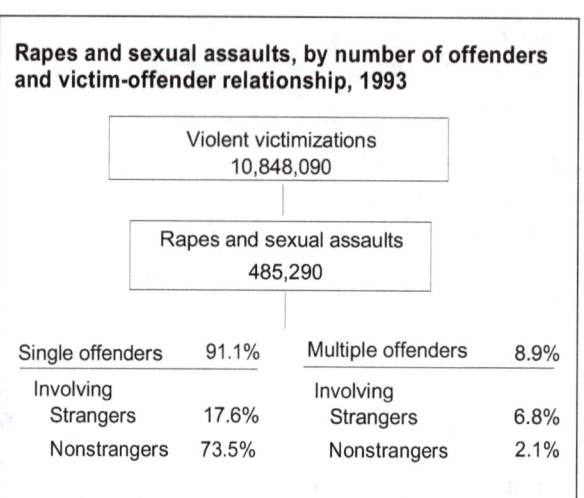

Rapes and sexual assaults, by number of offenders and victim-offender relationship, 1993

| Violent victimizations 10,848,090 |
| Rapes and sexual assaults 485,290 |

Single offenders	91.1%	Multiple offenders	8.9%
Involving		Involving	
Strangers	17.6%	Strangers	6.8%
Nonstrangers	73.5%	Nonstrangers	2.1%

Figure 4

‣About 4 in 10 rape/sexual assault incidents involved offenders who were age 30 or older, according to victims (figure 5). About a quarter of the incidents involved offenders under age 21.

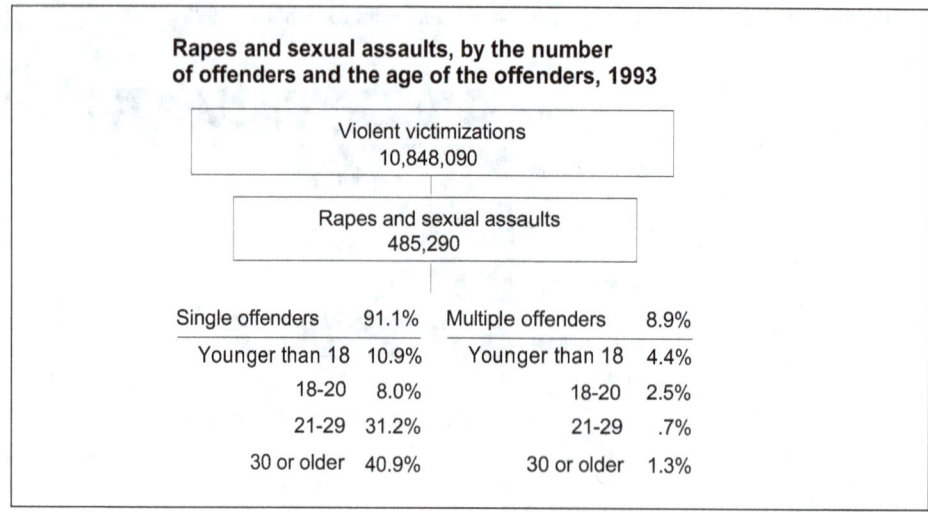

Rapes and sexual assaults, by the number of offenders and the age of the offenders, 1993

| Violent victimizations 10,848,090 |
| Rapes and sexual assaults 485,290 |

Single offenders	91.1%	Multiple offenders	8.9%
Younger than 18	10.9%	Younger than 18	4.4%
18-20	8.0%	18-20	2.5%
21-29	31.2%	21-29	.7%
30 or older	40.9%	30 or older	1.3%

Figure 5

Consequences of the rape/sexual assault victimization

▸About 7 out of 10 victims of rape/sexual assault reported that they took some form of self-protective action during the crime (figure 6). The most common form of self-defense was to resist by struggling or to chase and try to hold the offender.

▸Among victims who took a self-protective action, just over half felt that their actions helped the situation. About 1 in 5 victims felt that their actions either made the situation worse or simultaneously helped and worsened the situation.

▸Victims of rape/sexual assault accounted for about 4% of the victims of violence in 1993 but about 6% of the incidents in which some form of medical assistance was obtained.

▸About 1 in 11 rape/sexual assault victims reported that they suffered some economic loss as a consequence of the crime. The average economic loss was about $200, and nearly 7% of victims reported losing time from work.

Self-protective measures taken by victims of rape or sexual assault, 1993

Rape/sexual assault victimizations 485,290	

Victim took self-protective action 71.7%	Victim took no self-protective action 28.3%
Resisted or captured offender 19.3%	
Scared or warned offender 11.5%	
Persuaded or appeased offender 10.8%	
Ran away or hid 6.9%	
Attacked offender without weapon 6.1%	
Screamed from pain or fear 3.7%	
Got help or gave alarm 3.6%	
Other measures 9.8%	

Figure 6

The law enforcement response to rape and other sex offenses

In 1995, based on crimes recorded by law enforcement agencies nationwide, the number of forcible rapes per capita among women of all ages reported to law enforcement agencies was the lowest since 1985 (figure 7).

In addition to the NCVS, the Department of Justice obtains data on selected crimes *reported to* law enforcement authorities under the Uniform Crime Reports (UCR) program of the FBI. Begun in 1929, this program obtains annual counts of crime from more than 16,000 local, county, and State law enforcement agencies. The UCR selected offenses include murder and nonnegligent manslaughter, forcible rape, robbery, aggravated assault, burglary, larceny, motor vehicle theft, and arson.

Forcible rape in the UCR program is limited to incidents involving female victims. The UCR also obtains information from participating agencies on *arrests* for 21 additional categories of crime. The arrest tallies count arrests for sex offenses, including statutory rape and offenses against chastity, common decency, and morals. Commercialized vice and prostitution are excluded from this crime category. Forcible rape and sex offenses include attempts.

• Compared to 1990, the rate of rape among women in 1995 was 10% lower (80 per 100,000 women versus 72 per 100,000 women). In 1990 law enforcement agencies recorded about 1 rape for every 1,250 women, and in 1995, about 1 forcible rape for every 1,400 women.

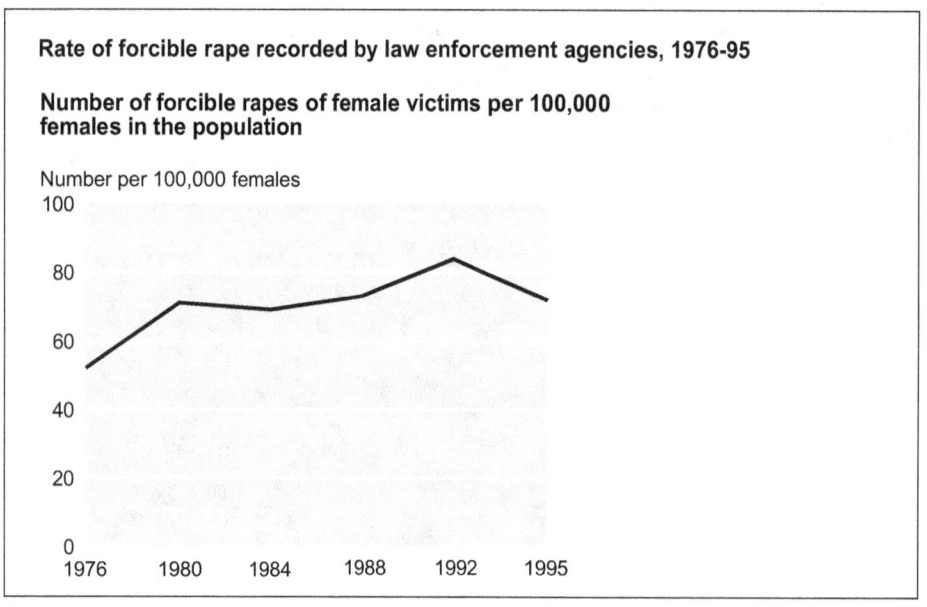

Rate of forcible rape recorded by law enforcement agencies, 1976-95

Number of forcible rapes of female victims per 100,000 females in the population

Number per 100,000 females

Figure 7

• The highest rate of forcible rape recorded by law enforcement agencies since 1976 was in 1992 — 84 per 100,000 women or about 1 forcible rape for every 1,200 women — and by 1995 the rate had decreased more than 14%.

• In 1992 police agencies recorded 109,060 forcible rapes nationwide; in 1995 the number of forcible rapes reported to the police was 97,460, the lowest total since 1989.

• Rates of forcible rape in 1995 range from 76 per 100,000 females in metropolitan areas to a rate of 49 per 100,000 female residents in rural counties. Over the last 10 years, substantial declines have occurred in the rate of forcible rape in metropolitan areas, while other areas, such as cities outside metropolitan areas (up 70%) and rural counties (up 40%), have experienced substantial growth in the per capita number of rapes brought to the attention of law enforcement authorities.

• In 1995, 87% of recorded forcible rapes were completed crimes and the remainder were classified as attempts. Law enforcement agencies indicated that about 8% of forcible rapes reported to them were determined to be unfounded and were excluded from the count of crimes.

• Law enforcement data indicate that the highest volume of rape reports in 1995 (9.9% of the annual total) were recorded in August and the fewest (6.8%) were recorded in December.

• In 1995 law enforcement agencies reported to the FBI that about half of all reported forcible rapes were cleared by an arrest. Jurisdictions of varying size had little difference in the clearance rate.

Arrests for forcible rape and other sex offenses

▸Law enforcement agencies in 1995 made an estimated 34,650 arrests for forcible rape and 94,500 arrests for other sex offenses (figure 8). The volume of arrests for rape and sex offenses peaked in 1991 at 148,120.

▸The per capita number of arrests for rape and other sex offenses in 1995 was the lowest recorded by law enforcement authorities since 1983. The per capita rate of arrest in 1995, 50.3 per 100,000 residents, is the same as the arrest rate in 1983.

▸In 1995, per capita arrest rates for rape were highest in States in the Midwest and lowest in Western States (figure 9).

▸By contrast, Western States had a substantially higher rate of arrest for other sex offenses. In the aggregate, the rate of arrest for sex offending (forcible rape + other sex offenses) translates into about 1 arrest for every 2,000 residents. In Western States, the region with the highest per capita number of arrests, the arrest rate equals about 1 arrest for every 1,745 residents.

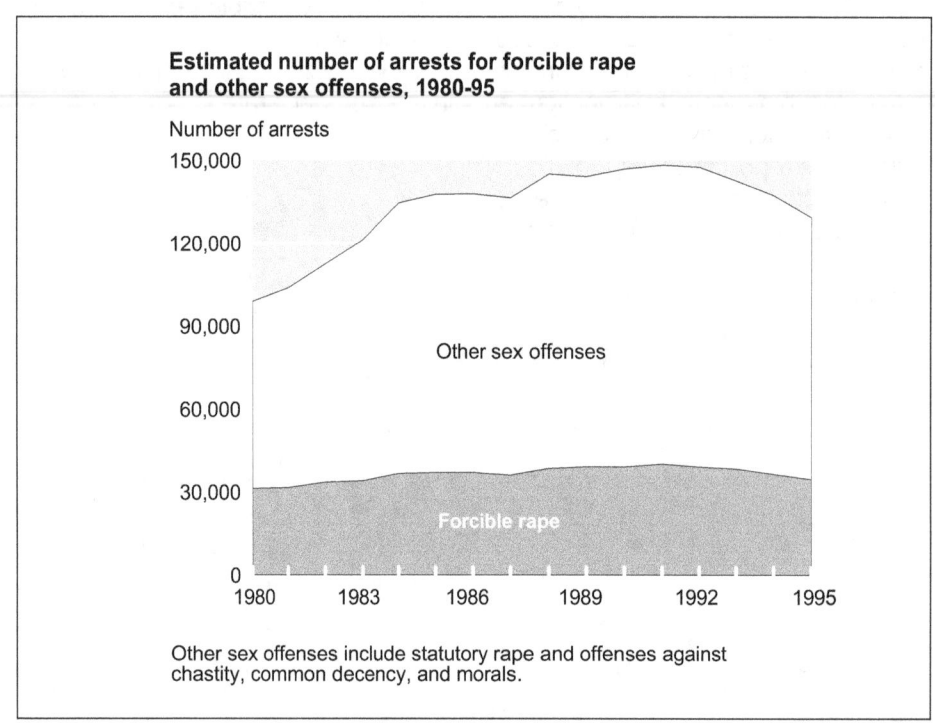

Figure 8

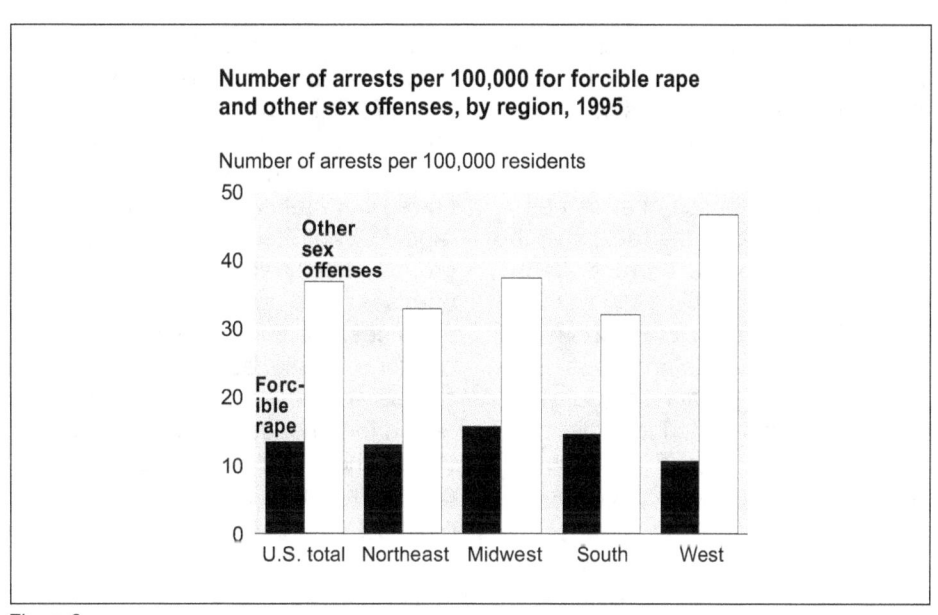

Number of arrests per 100,000 for forcible rape and other sex offenses, by region, 1995

Figure 9

► As with other types of violent crime, the size and type of jurisdiction are related to the rates of arrest for forcible rape and other sex offenses (figure 10). In 1995 cities with a population of 250,000 or more had aggregate arrest rates for rape and other sex offenses of about 80 per 100,000 — about 1 arrest for every 1,250 residents — 59% higher than the national average. By contrast, the lowest rates of arrest were recorded by law enforcement agencies in cities of 10,000 to 24,999 population — a rate of 36.9 per 100,000 residents or 1 arrest for every 2,700 residents. Rural and suburban counties and cities of less than 50,000 all had similar rates of arrest for rape and other sex offenses in 1995.

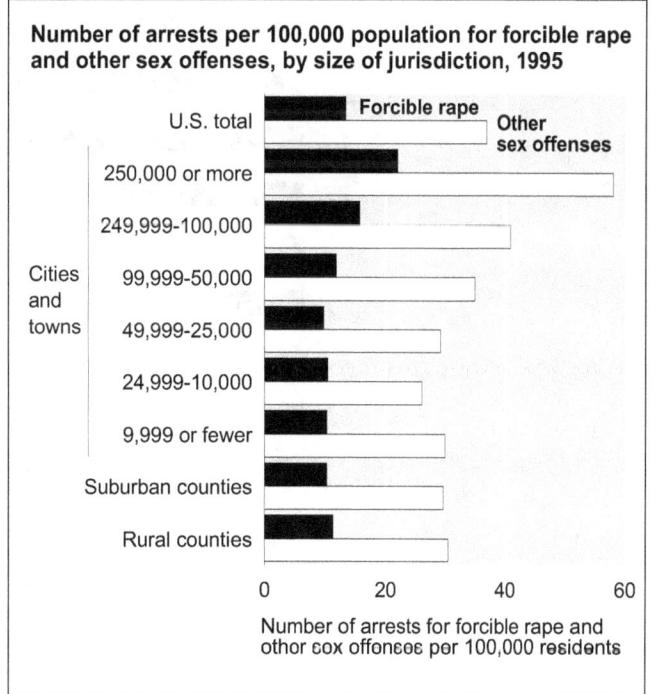

Number of arrests per 100,000 population for forcible rape and other sex offenses, by size of jurisdiction, 1995

Figure 10

▸Nearly all arrestees for forcible rape in 1995 were male (99%), while about 8% of arrestees for other sex offenses were female.

▸The racial distribution of arrestees for rape is similar to the racial distribution for all violent UCR arrests — 56% of arrestees for rape in 1995 were white, 42% were black, and 2% were of other races. White arrestees accounted for a substantially larger share of those arrested for other sex offenses, composing 75% of those arrested for these types of offenses in 1995.

▸Juveniles accounted for about 16% of forcible rape arrestees in 1995 and 17% of those arrested for other sex offenses (figure 11). Age and the type of sex offense for which an arrest occurred were related, with arrestees for rape concentrated in younger age groups while arrestees for other sex offenses more prevalent among older arrestees. Persons at least 50 years old, for example, accounted for 5% of rape arrestees but 10% of those arrested for other sex offenses. About a third of those arrested for rape and a quarter of those arrested for other sex offenses were in their twenties.

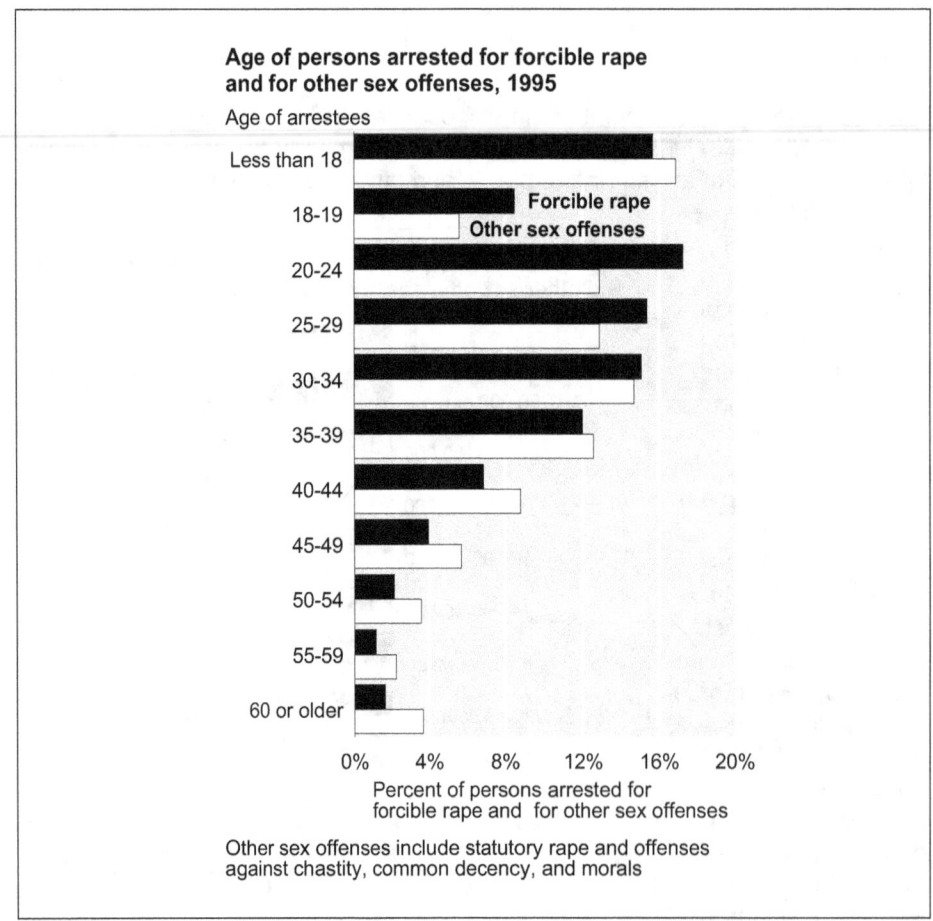

Figure 11

National Incident-Based Reporting System

The National Incident-Based Reporting System (NIBRS) represents the next generation of crime data from law enforcement agencies. It is designed to replace the nearly 70-year-old UCR program that compiles aggregate data on eight crimes. Rather than relying on a narrow group of 8 Index offenses, which are meant to convey the overall crime situation, NIBRS collects information on 57 types of crimes: 46 Group A crimes and 11 Group B crimes.

BJS received data tapes from the first NIBRS-participating States for calendar year 1991 — Alabama, North Dakota, and South Carolina. These three States account for about 3.3% of the U.S. population and 3.4% of rapes reported nationwide.

Sex of victim
About 10% of the rapes in the three States did not conform to the UCR definition of forcible rape — the victims were male (8.7% of rapes), the victim and offender were both female (0.8%), or the victim was male and the offender was female (0.2%).

Race of victim
Victims of rape were about evenly divided between whites and blacks; in about 88% of forcible rapes, the victim and offender were of the same race.

Age of victim
About 80% of rape victims were under age 30 — about half of these were under age 18. Victims younger than 12 accounted for 15% of those raped, and another 29% of rape victims were between 12 and 17.

Victim-offender relationship
For nearly 90% of the youngest victims of rape, those younger than 12, the offender was someone known to them. Law enforcement agencies reported that family members victimized 43% of these young victims — about 4 times the proportion found among victims age 30 or older (11%). Older victims (age 30 or above) were about 12 times as likely as the youngest victims to have been raped by a stranger (36% versus 3%).

About two-thirds of the victims age 18-29, the largest age group of rape victims, had a prior relationship with the rapist, but they were 7 times as likely to have been acquaintances (57%) as family members (8%).

Age of rapist
Just over 40% of the rapists were age 30 or older, about twice the percentage of victims of this age (20%). About 1 in 8 rapists was under 18. In 9 out of 10 rapes in which the offender was under 18, so was the victim.

Where rape occurred
Just over 60% of the rapes took place in a residence — about 1 in 3 rapes by a stranger and 9 in 10 rapes by a family member.

When rape occurred
Across the 3 States, an average of 8 rapes a day took place, ranging from 11 on Saturdays to 6 on Wednesdays. Nearly a third of the rapes took place between midnight and 4 a.m., with little variation in time of day by victim-offender relationship or by location of occurrence. The period from 8 p.m. Friday to 8 a.m. Saturday held the largest number of rapes in a 12-hour block reported by the NIBRS participants.

Weapons

About 12% of rapes involved the use of a gun (5%) or knife (7%), and 80% involved the use of physical force only.

Offenders were 5 times more likely to use a gun in the rape of a stranger (10%) than in the rape of a family member (2%). About 8% of rapes by ex-spouses involved a gun, and another 12%, a knife.

Rapes with black offenders and black victims were about twice as likely as white-on-white rapes to involve the use of a gun or knife (14% versus 7%), but inter-racial rapes, black-on-white or white-on-black, were equally likely to involve the use of a gun or knife (about 22%).

Roadways or alleys were the most likely places where a rapist used a gun (13%).

Injuries

About 40% of rape victims suffered a collateral injury — 5% suffered a major injury such as severe lacerations, fractures, internal injuries, or unconsciousness.

More than half of spousal rapes, rapes by ex-spouses, and stranger rapes resulted in victim injury, while about a quarter of parent-child rapes resulted in major injury. Injuries were most common among victims age 30 or older and victims of rapists armed with a knife. Nearly 6 in 10 rapes involving a knife resulted in victim injury.

Based on data from 6 States in 1990, about half of those arrested for rape were convicted. For 4 in 10 arrestees, the conviction was for a felony.

Arrestees for rape
100%

Rape arrestees for whom felony prosecution was sought
80%

Convicted	48%		Not convicted	32%
Felony	40%		Dismissed	29%
Misdemeanor	6%		Acquitted	2%
Other	2%		Other	1%

This analysis from *Tracking Offenders 1990* (NCJ 148200) retrospectively tracked case processing of rape defendants after disposition in 1990. The analysis used more than 527,000 felony arrests, of which 4,175 were for rape.

Figure 12

Pretrial release and adjudication of rape offenders

About 5 out of 10 rape defendants are released prior to trial, and 8 out of 10 convicted rape defendants had entered a guilty plea to the offense.

Every other year BJS obtains longitudinal case processing data on a sample of felony defendants representing the Nation's 75 most populous counties. The defendants' cases are tracked for 1 year following the filing of felony charges by the prosecutor. The counties account for about a third of the U.S. population but about half of all reported crime and about half of all felony convictions nationwide.

The most recently published survey findings are drawn from information collected on 13,206 felony cases filed in May 1992 representing more than 55,000 felony cases filed that month. An estimated 1.4% of the felony filings were for rape.

Data on the sentencing of convicted felons are also collected biennially under the BJS National Judicial Reporting Program (NJRP). This survey obtains information from a nationally representative sample of counties about the sentences that felons receive in State courts, the methods by which convictions were obtained, and the types and duration of sentences imposed, as well as any contingent requirements associated with sentences.

The most recently available data are drawn from the 1992 annual collection, which covered 300 counties and detailed data on 105,657 felony defendants. An estimated 2.4% of the convicted felons had been convicted of rape.

In both collection programs, rape is the only sex offense category for which data are separately reported. Also in both series, rape victims can include males and females.

Processing of rape defendants before disposition of their case

• About 1 in 20 filings for a violent felony (or 1.4% of all felony filings) in the 75 largest counties in 1992 were for

Table 1. Pretrial release of rape defendants in large urban counties		
	Defendants	
	All violent offenses	Rape
Total	100%	100%
Released prior to trial	58	48
Financial release	25	24
Nonfinancial release	33	24
Detained until disposition	42	52
Median bail amount set	$10,000	$23,500

rape. That same year, there were about 6 times as many felony filings for robbery, 9 times as many felony filings for assault, and 21 times as many filings for felony drug offenses.

• An estimated 48% of rape defendants were released from detention prior to the disposition of their case (table 1). The rate of release pending disposition of a rape charge was lower than that for other violent felonies: Only defendants charged with murder had a lower rate of release (24%) than those for whom rape charges were pending. An estimated 3% of all rape defendants had no bail amount set and were not eligible for release pending the outcome of their case. An estimated 49% of rape defendants had bail set but were unable to post sufficient collateral to secure release.

• About half of felony rape defendants who secured release posted financial collateral, and the other half obtained release through nonfinancial means.

• The most common methods used by those charged with rape for securing financial release were obtaining a surety bond (12% of all defendants) that involved a promissory note from a bail bondsman, posting a deposit bond that is a percentage of the set bail (6% of all defendants), paying the full cash bail amount required (4%), or posting property as collateral (1%).

• The most commonly used method of nonfinancial release was release on personal recognizance (11% of all rape defendants), which is a promise to appear as required by the court. An estimated 9% of all rape defendants were released on some form of conditional release or supervised release pending disposition of their case, a method that normally entails supervision by a pretrial services agency under special conditions set by the court. Small percentages of rape defendants were also released by an unsecured bond or due to a crowding emergency in the jail.

• The court set bail for an estimated 73% of rape defendants. The median bail for rape defendants was $23,500, about $50,000 less than the median bail set for murder defendants and $13,500 more than the median bail accorded robbery defendants. Among rape defendants securing release, the median bail was $10,000; among rape defendants failing to secure release, the median bail was $25,000.

Sentencing of convicted rape defendants

• In 1992 an estimated 21,655 felony defendants nationwide were convicted of rape (figure 13). For about 14%, the conviction followed a jury trial, but for most defendants (82%), conviction followed a guilty plea. The remainder, 4%, were convicted following a bench trial.

• Overall, just over two-thirds of convicted rape defendants received a prison sentence. An additional 19% of convicted rape defendants were sentenced to a term in a local jail, and about 13% received a sentence to probation supervision in the community.

• For rape defendants sentenced to prison, the average term imposed was 164 months, or just under 14 years. The average jail term for an offender convicted of rape was 8 months, and the average probation term was just under 6 years. An estimated 2% of convicted rapists received a term of life imprisonment.

• About a third of rape defendants had one or more additional felony convictions collateral to the conviction for rape. Collateral convictions were associated with an increased probability of receiving a prison sentence.

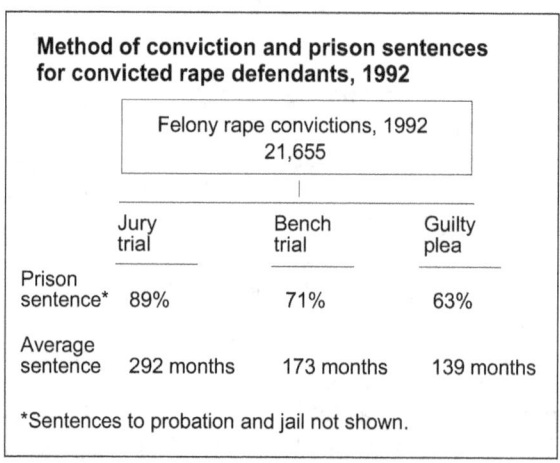

Method of conviction and prison sentences for convicted rape defendants, 1992

Felony rape convictions, 1992
21,655

	Jury trial	Bench trial	Guilty plea
Prison sentence*	89%	71%	63%
Average sentence	292 months	173 months	139 months

*Sentences to probation and jail not shown.

Figure 13

- Sentences of convicted rape defendants also carried additional penalties, which included a fine (13% of convicted defendants), victim restitution (12%), required treatment (10%), community service (2%), and other penalties (10%).

- The method of conviction affected both the probability of receiving a prison sentence and the term of imprisonment for rape. Defendants convicted by a jury were substantially more likely to receive a prison term than those convicted in bench trials or by plea, and the term was substantially longer. The average prison term for rape following a jury conviction was nearly 13 years longer than the average sentence received by those pleading guilty to rape.

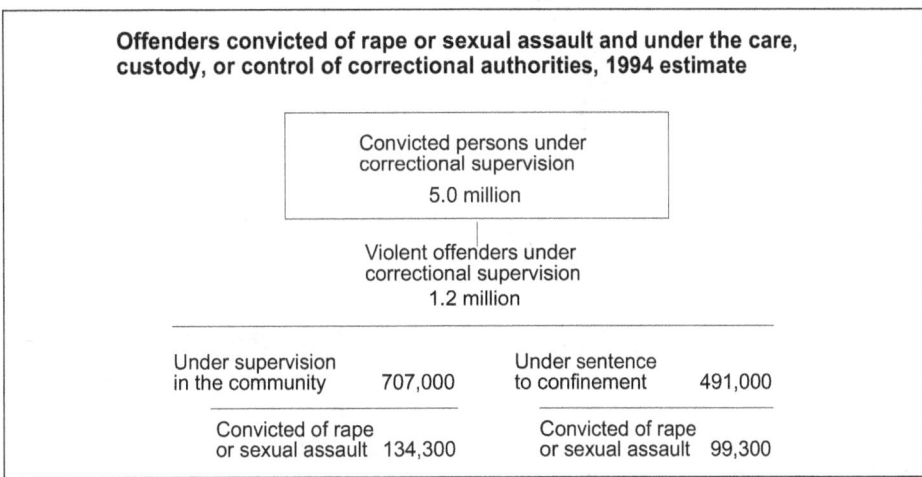

Offenders convicted of rape or sexual assault and under the care, custody, or control of correctional authorities, 1994 estimate

Convicted persons under correctional supervision

5.0 million

Violent offenders under correctional supervision

1.2 million

| Under supervision in the community | 707,000 | Under sentence to confinement | 491,000 |

| Convicted of rape or sexual assault | 134,300 | Convicted of rape or sexual assault | 99,300 |

Figure 14

Corrections and the convicted sex offender

On a given day there are approximately 234,000 offenders convicted of rape or sexual assault under the care, custody, or control of corrections agencies; nearly 60% of these sex offenders are under conditional supervision in the community.

Data on sentenced sex offenders are obtained under a wide variety of BJS statistical programs covering both community-based and institutional corrections.

BJS has conducted annual counts of the probation and parole populations since 1978, collecting the number entering and leaving, population characteristics, and the end-of-year counts. Probation and parole agencies supervise about three-quarters of the correctional population in the United States.

In 1991 BJS carried out the first full census since 1976 of the nearly 5,000 probation and parole agencies and offices. The census obtained detailed information on the population under supervision and the resources available to manage the correctional populations in the community. This effort

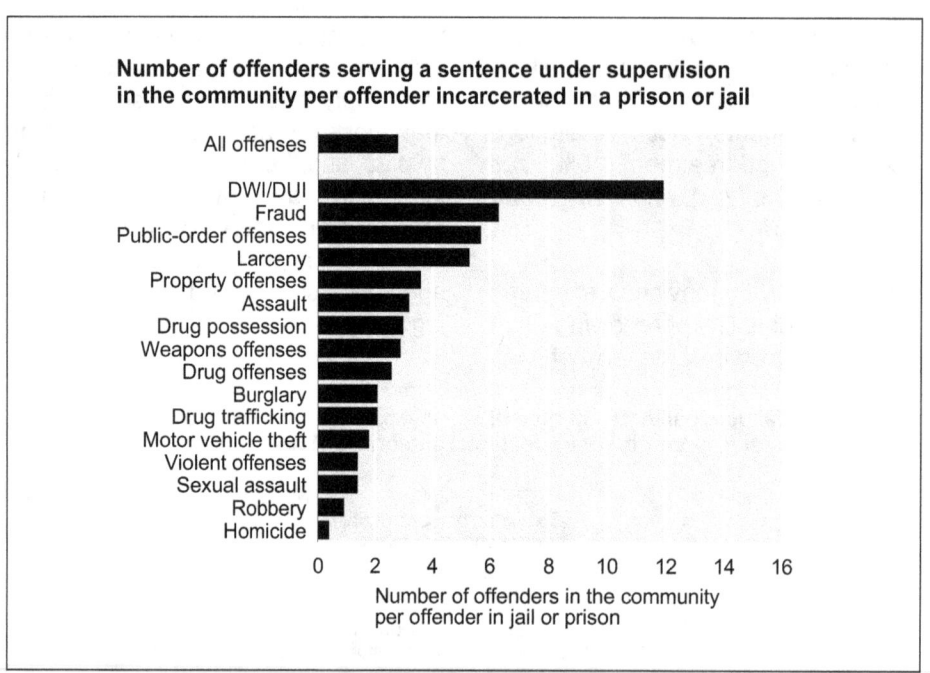

Number of offenders serving a sentence under supervision in the community per offender incarcerated in a prison or jail

All offenses

DWI/DUI
Fraud
Public-order offenses
Larceny
Property offenses
Assault
Drug possession
Weapons offenses
Drug offenses
Burglary
Drug trafficking
Motor vehicle theft
Violent offenses
Sexual assault
Robbery
Homicide

0   2   4   6   8   10   12   14   16

Number of offenders in the community
per offender in jail or prison

Figure 15

also provided the first-ever national information on the offense composition of community supervision populations.

In 1995 BJS conducted the first national survey of offenders on probation, gathering detailed demographic data as well as information on prior record, drug use history, use of weapons, and victim attributes. BJS expects to publish the results of the survey in early 1997.

Populations confined in local jails and State and Federal prisons account for about a quarter of the total population under correctional sanction. As with probation and parole, annual collection programs on institutional corrections detail a variety of characteristics associated with the confined population, including admissions and releases, demographic composition, and the count on a specified day.

Since the early 1970's, BJS has carried out facility censuses of both prisons and jails. In addition, periodic BJS self-report surveys of nationally representative samples of prison and jail inmates provide data on offender characteristics not normally available in official institutional records, such as drug and alcohol use patterns, family, background, and the characteristics of victims. BJS also collects individual-level information from prison and parole authorities on those admitted to and released from their custody, providing important national information on sentence lengths and time served prior to discharge.

• Based upon the most recent data available from these series, it is estimated that rape and sexual assault offenders account for nearly 4% of those on probation, about 3% of convicted offenders in local jails, about 10% of those serving time in State prisons, about 1% of those serving time in Federal prisons, and about 4% of those on parole supervision in the community.

• Rape and sexual assault offenders account for about 6% of those entering State prisons, less than 5% of those discharged from State prisons, just over 4% of admissions to parole supervision, and less than 4% of those discharged from parole supervision. In the aggregate, rape and sexual assault offenders account for just under 5% of the entire population under correctional sanction on a given day (figure 14).

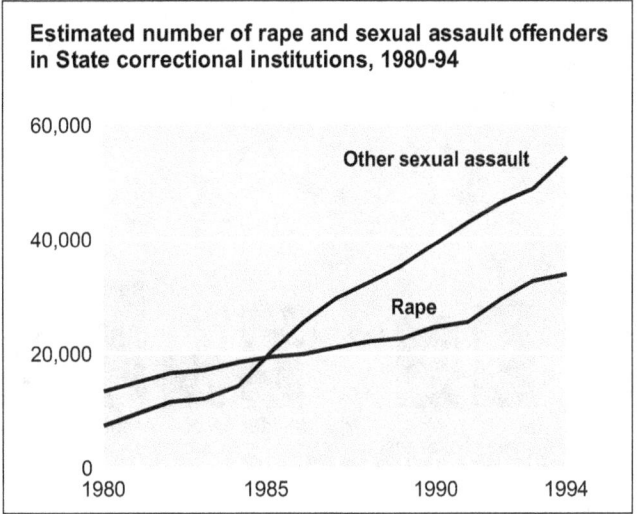

Estimated number of rape and sexual assault offenders in State correctional institutions, 1980-94

Figure 16

	Convicted offenders, estimated, 1994		
	Total population	Sex offenders Number	Percent
Probation	2,964,171	106,710	3.6%
Jail	304,274	10,345	3.4%
State prisons	906,112	88,100	9.7%
Federal prisons	87,515	875	1.0%
Parole	690,159	27,606	4.0%
Total	4,952,231	233,636	4.7%

• For each convicted offender in a prison or jail, there are nearly 3 offenders under probation or parole supervision in the community (figure 15).

For those convicted of rape or sexual assault, the ratio of those on conditional release to those incarcerated is 1.4 to 1.

• In 1980 State prisons held 295,819 persons in their custody, of which an estimated 20,500, or 6.9%, had been convicted of rape or sexual assault.[2] By 1994, the State prison population had increased to 906,112, of which 88,000, or 9.7%, were sex offenders. While the prison population increased 206% over the period, the number of imprisoned sex offenders grew 330% (figure 16).

[2]*Sexual assault* includes convictions for statutory rape, forcible sodomy, lewd acts with children, and other conviction offenses related to fondling, molestation, or indecent practices. The term *sex offender* describes those offenders convicted of rape or sexual assault.

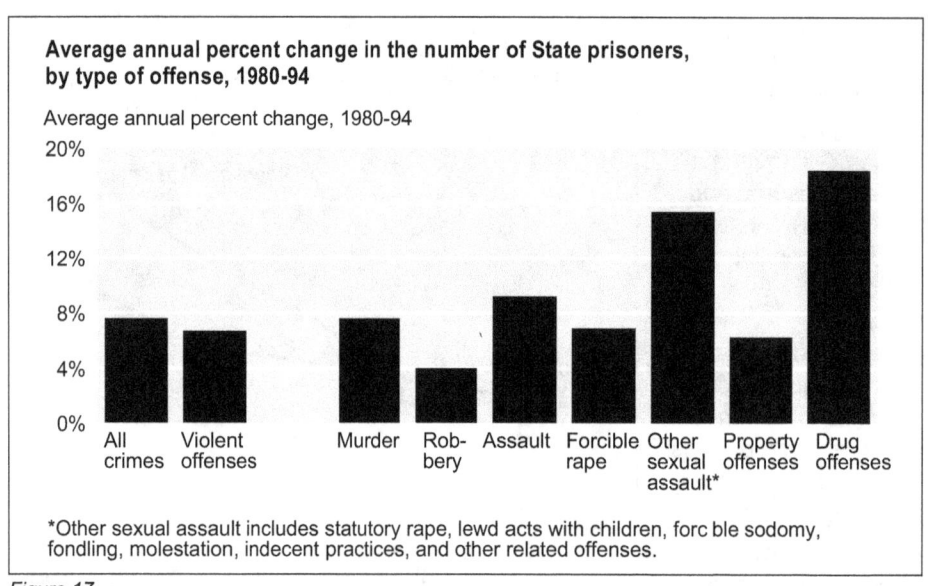

Average annual percent change in the number of State prisoners, by type of offense, 1980-94

Average annual percent change, 1980-94

*Other sexual assault includes statutory rape, lewd acts with children, forc ble sodomy, fondling, molestation, indecent practices, and other related offenses.

Figure 17

• From 1980 to 1994 the average annual growth in the number of prisoners was 7.6% (figure 17). Inmates serving time for drug offenses experienced the highest annual rate of increase with an average of about 18% per year after 1980. However, inmates imprisoned for sexual assaults other than rape experienced the second fastest rise, increasing by an annual average of more than 15% — a more rapid rate of change than for any other category of violent crime.

• The number of imprisoned rapists grew at a yearly average of about 7% over the 14 years.

• Even with the comparatively higher growth rate of prisoners serving time for sexual assault, the absolute increase in their numbers between 1980 and 1994 was from 7,300 to 54,300, accounting for just under 8% of the total increase in the State prison population over the period.

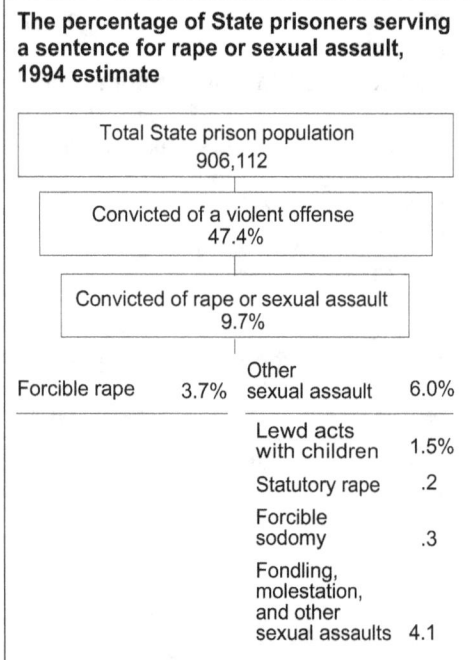

The percentage of State prisoners serving a sentence for rape or sexual assault, 1994 estimate

Total State prison population
906,112

Convicted of a violent offense
47.4%

Convicted of rape or sexual assault
9.7%

Forcible rape	3.7%	
Other sexual assault		6.0%
Lewd acts with children		1.5%
Statutory rape		.2
Forcible sodomy		.3
Fondling, molestation, and other sexual assaults		4.1

Figure 18

• In 1994 there were an estimated 88,100 sex offenders incarcerated in State prisons nationwide, accounting for about 9.7% of the inmate population (figure 18). Sex offenders accounted for about 1 in 5 violent offenders housed in State prisons in 1994. About 6 out of 10 sex offenders had been convicted of sexual assault, and 4 in 10 had been convicted of forcible rape. The largest category of sex offenders was composed of those serving time for molestation, fondling, or other related kinds of sexual assault.

• Over the period from 1985 to 1993, there has been only slight variation in the average sentence received for rape and sexual assault by those entering State prisons (figure 19). Entering prisoners convicted of rape have received sentences averaging between 12 and 13 years, while those convicted of sexual assault have been admitted to prison with sentences averaging between 8 and 9 years. There is no evidence from national data on those admitted to State prisons that the average sentence for either category of crime has been lengthening.

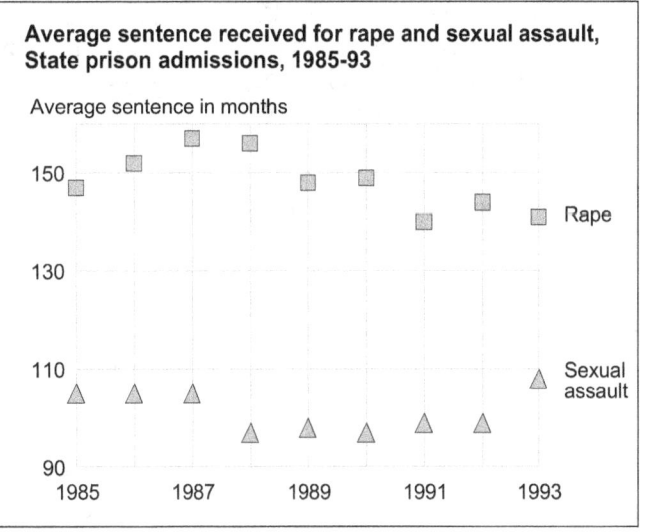

Average sentence received for rape and sexual assault, State prison admissions, 1985-93

Figure 19

• National data on sex offenders discharged from State prisons between 1985 and 1993 reveal two distinct trends:
  - an increase in the average length of stay
  - an increase in the percentage of the sentence served in confinement prior to release.

• While the average sentence of convicted rapists discharged from State prisons has remained stable at approximately 10 years, the average time served has increased from about 3½ years to about 5 years, raising the percentage of sentence served from about 38% to about 50% (figure 20).

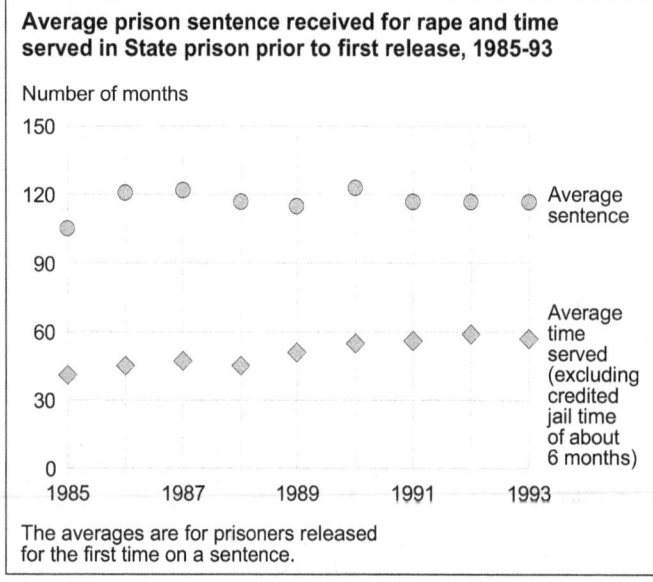

Average prison sentence received for rape and time served in State prison prior to first release, 1985-93

Number of months

The averages are for prisoners released for the first time on a sentence.

Figure 20

• For those exiting prison after serving time for convictions for sexual assault, the average sentence they had received remained stable at about 6½ years, while the average time served grew by about 6 months, from just over 2 years to just under 3 years. Released sexual assaulters in 1985 had served about 34% of their sentences prior to discharge; sexual assaulters released in 1993 had served just over 41% of their sentences (figure 21).

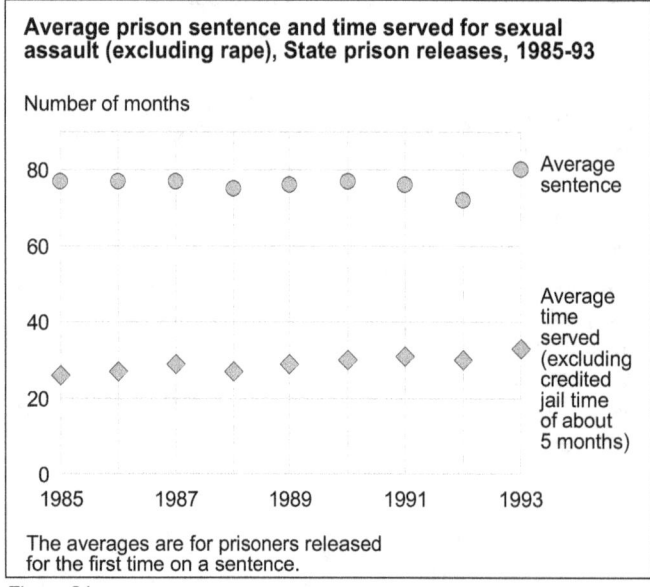

Average prison sentence and time served for sexual assault (excluding rape), State prison releases, 1985-93

Number of months

The averages are for prisoners released for the first time on a sentence.

Figure 21

Characteristics of imprisoned rape and sexual assault offenders

• Imprisoned violent sex offenders were more likely to have been male and white than other violent offenders (table 2). Offenders serving time for sexual assault, in contrast to those incarcerated for rape, were substantially more likely to be white, and they were nearly 3 years older, on average, at the time of their arrest for the offense. While about half of incarcerated rapists were white, about 3 out of 4 prisoners serving time for sexual assault were white.

• Age differences were particularly striking — less than 5% of incarcerated violent offenders are at least age 50, but about 7% of rapists and 12% of sexual assaulters are 50 or older. The average age at arrest of violent offenders serving time in State prisons was 29 years, compared to rapists, 31 years, and sexual assaulters, 34 years.

Table 2. Characteristics of imprisoned rape and sexual assault offenders

| | Offenders in State prison | | |
Characteristic	All violent	Rape	Sexual assault
Estimated number of offenders, 1994	429,400	33,800	54,300
Sex			
Male	96.2%	99.6%	98.8%
Female	3.8	.4	1.2
Race			
White	48.1%	52.2%	73.9%
Black	48.2	43.7	22.8
Other	3.7	4.1	3.3
Age at arrest for current offense			
Less than 18	3.1%	.6%	1.1%
18-24	38.1	33.7	23.6
25-29	22.1	20.9	17.0
30-34	15.0	17.7	16.3
35-39	8.8	10.9	13.4
40-44	5.0	4.1	10.2
45-49	3.4	4.8	6.6
50-54	1.7	2.9	4.4
55-59	1.5	3.2	4.2
60 or older	1.4	1.3	3.2
Average at arrest	29 yrs	31 yrs	34 yrs
Marital status			
Married	17.1%	22.1%	21.8%
Widowed	2.6	1.2	1.7
Divorced	21.4	28.5	35.0
Separated	5.6	6.2	4.9
Never married	53.3	42.0	36.6

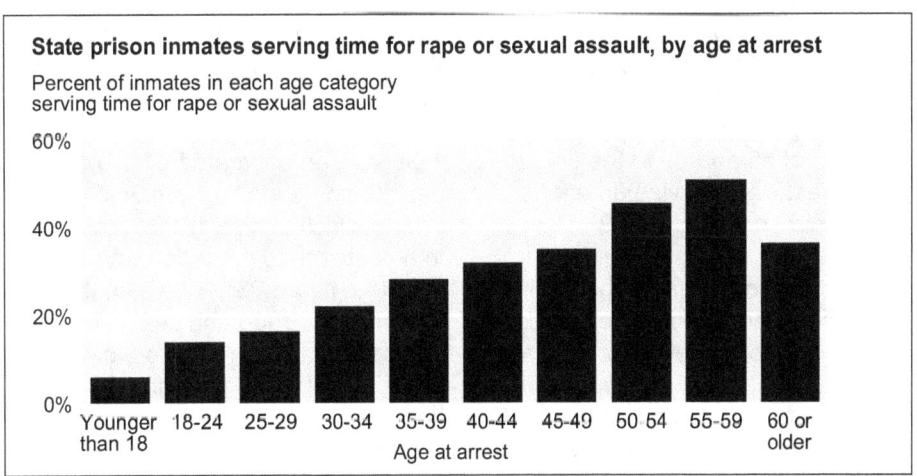

State prison inmates serving time for rape or sexual assault, by age at arrest

Percent of inmates in each age category serving time for rape or sexual assault

Figure 22

Conviction histories of offenders serving time in State prisons for rape or sexual assault, 1994 estimates

In 1994, in the custody of State correctional authorities
906,112 offenders

Serving time in State prisons for a violent offense
429,000 offenders

Serving time for rape and sexual assault
88,100 offenders

	Forc ble rape	Statutory rape	Lewd acts with children	Forc ble sodomy	Other sexual assaults
Number of inmates	33,800	1,450	13,400	2,500	36,900
Prior convictions	64%	56%	55%	70%	59%
Prior convictions for violence	26%	31%	22%	32%	26%
Prior convictions for rape or sexual assault	**10%**	**26%**	**17%**	**20%**	**12%**

Figure 23

• The relationship between age at arrest and the likelihood of having been imprisoned for a violent sex offense is also shown by the percentage of each age group serving time for such offenses. While about 1 in 7 inmates arrested between the ages of 18 and 24 had been incarcerated for rape or sexual assault, half of those between the ages of 55 and 59 at the time of their arrest were serving time for a violent sex crime (figure 22).

• In addition to race and age differences between sex offenders and other violent offenders, substantial differences in marital status backgrounds are also evident. Less than half (47%) of prisoners serving time for violence report ever having been married.

About 6 in 10 rapists and more than 6 in 10 sexual assaulters reported having ever been married. Similar to other violent offenders, however, about a third of those who reported that they had ever married indicated that they were married at the time of their imprisonment.

• Overall, an estimated 61% of violent sex offenders in State prisons have a prior conviction history that resulted in a sentence to probation or incarceration (figure 23). An estimated 1 in 4 imprisoned rape and sexual assault offenders has a prior history of convictions for violent crimes, and 1 in 7 had been previously convicted of a violent sex crime.

• Rapists and sexual assaulters serving time in State prisons were less likely to have had a prior conviction history or a history of violence than other incarcerated violent offenders. However, they were substantially more likely to have had a history of convictions for violent sex offenses — imprisoned sex offenders, while accounting for about 20% of all violent offenders, accounted for about 66% of all violent offenders with a prior history of sex offenses.

Prior convictions	Offenders in State prison		
	All violent	Rape	Sexual assault
Any felony	71%	64%	58%
Violence	31%	26%	25%
Sex offenses	4%	10%	15%

• Sexual assault offenders were substantially more likely than any other category of offenders to report having experienced physical or sexual abuse while growing up (figure 24). However, two-thirds of sexual assault offenders reported that they had never been physically or sexually abused as a child.

• About 14% of imprisoned sex offenders reported that their sentence included a special court condition that they receive psychological or specialized sex-offender treatment. Overall, about 4% of the sentences of confined violent offenders had a similar requirement.

The victims of imprisoned rape and sexual assault offenders

• Imprisoned rape offenders were more likely than those convicted of sexual assault to report having had a single victim for the offense for which they were serving time.

Number of victims	Offenders in State prison		
	All violent	Rape	Sexual assault
1	76.1%	85.9%	78.8%
2 or more	23.9%	14.1%	21.2%

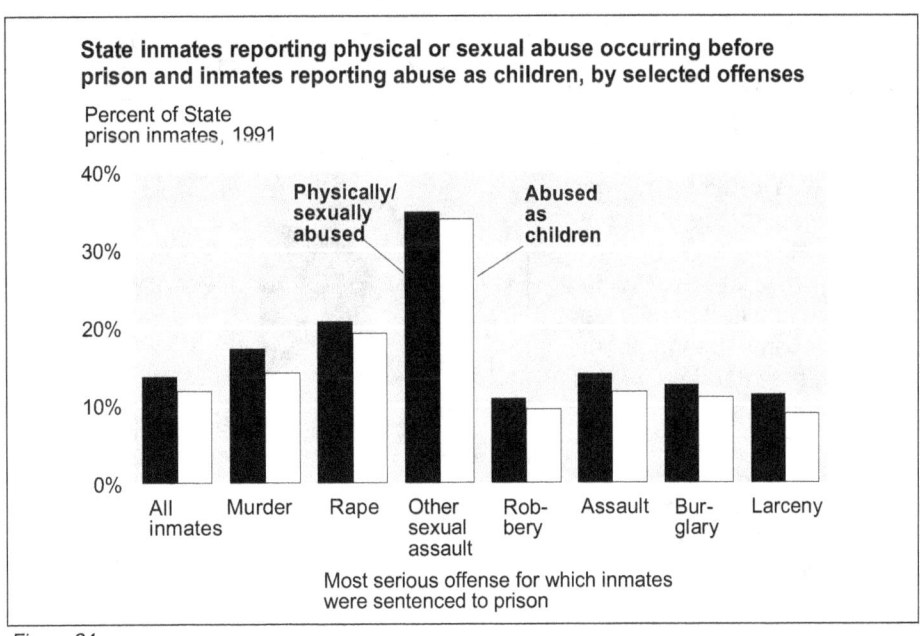

State inmates reporting physical or sexual abuse occurring before prison and inmates reporting abuse as children, by selected offenses

Percent of State prison inmates, 1991

Figure 24

• Sexual assault offenders were about 3 times as likely as those serving time for rape to have had a male victim (table 3). Both categories of violent sex offenders, however, reported that the vast majority of their victims had been female.

• The victims of sexual assault, like the offenders, were more likely to have been white than was the case among victims and offenders in rape and other violent crimes.

• Violent sex offenders with single victims reported that two-thirds of their victims had been under the age of 18 (figures 25 and 26). About 4 in 10 rapists reported their victim had been a child, and 8 out of 10 sexual assaulters said their victim had been less than 18 years old. Victims of sexual assault were the youngest victims among those persons described by incarcerated violent State prisoners. The median age of the victims of imprisoned sexual assaulters was less than 13 years old; the median age of rape victims was about 22 years.

• While nearly half of all violent offenders committed the crime for which they had been imprisoned against a stranger, about 30% of rapists and less than 15% of sexual assaulters reported their victim had been a stranger to them. Sexual assaulters were about 3 times as likely as all violent offenders

Table 3. Victims of imprisoned rape and sexual assault offenders

| Characteristic | Violent offenders in State prison reporting single victims | | |
	All	Rape	Sexual assault
Sex of victim			
Male	55.8%	5.5%	15.2%
Female	44.2	94.5	84.8
Race of victim			
White	64.5%	67.8%	76.4%
Black	29.8	27.6	20.1
Other	5.7	4.6	3.5
Age of victim			
12 or younger	9.9%	15.2%	44.7%
13 to 17	8.8	21.8	33.0
18 to 24	17.5	25.1	9.4
25 to 34	31.1	25.4	7.7
35 to 54	26.5	10.2	4.3
55 or older	6.3	2.3	.9
Median age	29 yrs	22 yrs	13 yrs
Relationship to offender			
Family	12.9%	20.3%	37.7%
Spouse	2.5	1.2	.6
Child/stepchild	6.1	14.0	25.9
Other relative	4.3	5.1	11.2
Intimate	5.5	9.1	6.2
Boyfriend/girlfriend	5.0	8.8	5.4
Ex-spouse	.5	.3	.8
Acquaintance	34.7	40.8	41.2
Stranger	46.9	29.8	14.9

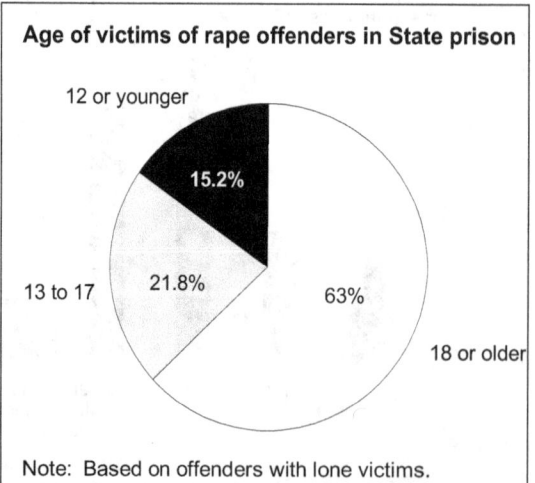

Age of victims of rape offenders in State prison

12 or younger — 15.2%
13 to 17 — 21.8%
18 or older — 63%

Note: Based on offenders with lone victims.

Figure 25

and twice as likely as rapists to report that the victim had been a member of their family. For 1 in 4 imprisoned sexual assaulters, the victim had been their own child or stepchild.

• Violent sex offenders convicted of rape or sexual assault were substantially less likely than other violent offenders to have used a weapon during the commission of the crime (table 4). This difference is especially evident for firearms: About 30% of all violent offenders reported having used a firearm, while about 5% of rapists and 2% of sexual assaulters used a firearm during the crime. However, rapists were about as likely as all violent offenders to report having used a knife while committing the crime.

Recidivism of violent sex offenders

• About 45% of State prisoners participating in the 1991 survey had committed the crime for which they were serving a sentence while in the community on probation or parole. These

Table 4. Inmate reports of their weapon use in violent crime

| | Violent offenders in State prison | | |
	All	Rape	Sexual assault
Total	100%	100%	100%
Any weapon	45.7%	16.6%	5.6%
Handgun	24.2	4.7	1.5
Other firearm	5.8	.7	.5
Knife	11.1	9.6	3.1
Other weapon	4.7	1.6	.5
No weapon	54.3	83.4	94.4

offenders were convicted of about 13,000 rapes out of nearly 91,000 convictions for violence during the period preceding imprisonment when they had been under supervision in the community.

• Violent sex offenders in State prisons were less likely than violent offenders overall to have been on probation or parole prior to prison admission. As a group, about 1 in 5 sex offenders reported that they had been under conditional supervision in the community prior to entering prison.

• An estimated 24% of those serving time for rape and 19% of those serving time for sexual assault had been on probation or parole at the time of the offense for which they were in State prison in 1991.

• A 3-year BJS followup of a sample of felony offenders placed on probation found that rapists had a lower rate of re-arrest for a new felony and a lower rate of re-arrest for a violent felony than most

Age of victims of sexual assault offenders in State prison

18 or olde

22.3%

12 or younger

44.7%

33%

13 to 17

Note: Based on offenders with lone victims.

Figure 26

categories of probationers with convictions for violence. While about 41% of violent probationers were re-arrested within 3 years of placement on probation for a new felony offense, an estimated 19.5% of rapists were re-arrested for a new felony within 3 years.

• Rapists on probation were more likely than other felons, however, to be re-arrested for a new rape. While about 1.5% of violent felony probationers were re-arrested for a new rape within 3 years, about 3% of probationers under conditional supervision after conviction for rape were re-arrested for a new rape within 3 years.

• BJS also carried out a 3-year followup of a sample drawn to represent 109,000 prisoners released in 1983 from prisons in 11 States. During the followup period, this group of releasees acquired about 50,000 arrests for new violent crimes, including nearly 4,000 arrests for rape and sexual assault. Prior to their imprisonment, fingerprint records for this group of offenders evidenced more than 19,000 prior arrests for rape and sexual assault.

• Offenders convicted of rape and sexual assault composed just over 4% of those discharged from prisons in the 11 States in 1983. Over the 3-year period following prison release, an estimated 52% of discharged rapists and 48% of discharged sexual assaulters were re-arrested for a new crime. Their criminal history records also evidenced a lower percentage of sex offenders who were reconvicted and reimprisoned during the followup

period than was the case for all violent offenders discharged from prison.

| Offenders | Percent of all inmates | | |
	Re-arrested	Recon-victed	Reincar-cerated
All violent	60%	42%	37%
Rape	52%	36%	32%
Sexual assault	48%	33%	24%

• During the followup period, which began in 1983, the prison release cohort accounted for 3.8% of all the rape arrests that took place in the 11 States in 1983, 2.4% of all the rape arrests in the 11 States in 1984, and about 1% of the arrests for rape in the 11 States in 1985 and 1986.

• Nearly 28% of released rapists were re-arrested for a new violent crime within 3 years (figure 27). For nearly 8% of released rapists, the new arrest for a violent crime was another charge for rape. During the followup period

Re-arrests of convicted rapists released from prison and followed for 3 years

Convicted rapists released from prison and followed for 3 years
2,214

Re-arrested for a new crime
51.5%

Re-arrested for a new violent crime
27.5%

| Murder | Rape | Robbery | Assault |
| 2.8% | 7.7% | 8.5% | 10.7% |

This BJS study tracked a sample of offenders in 11 States drawn to represent those released from prisons in those States in 1983. Each offender was tracked through both State and Federal criminal history records. Offenders may have been arrested more than once during the followup period.

Figure 27

about 1% of murderers, robbers, and assaulters were rearrested for a new rape. Released rapists were found to be 10.5 times as likely as nonrapists to be re-arrested for rape, and those who had served time for sexual assault were 7.5 times as likely as those convicted of other crimes to be re-arrested for a new sexual assault.

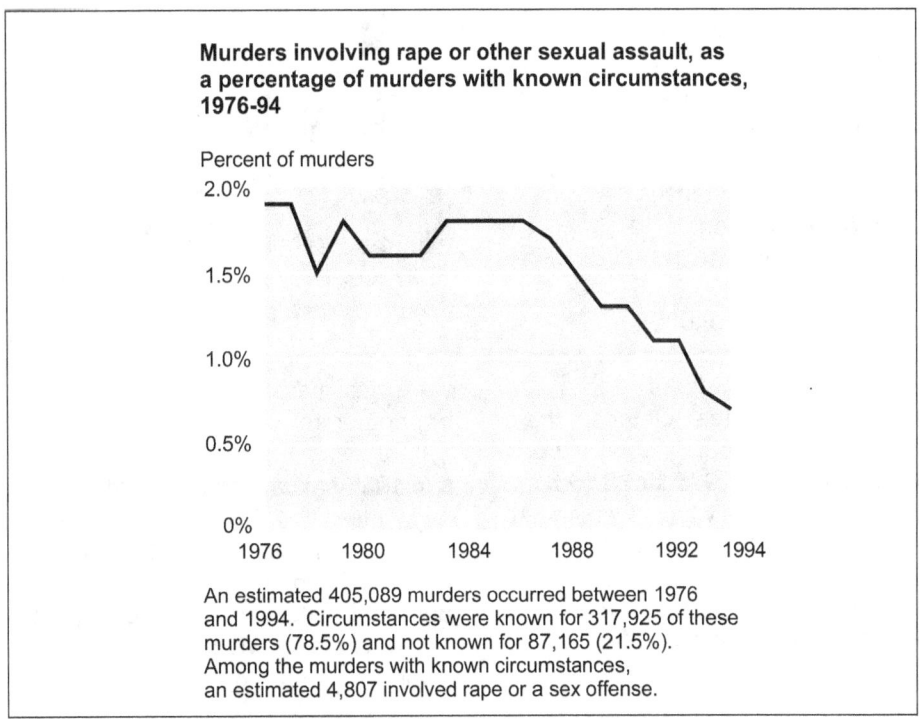

Murders involving rape or other sexual assault, as a percentage of murders with known circumstances, 1976-94

Percent of murders

An estimated 405,089 murders occurred between 1976 and 1994. Circumstances were known for 317,925 of these murders (78.5%) and not known for 87,165 (21.5%). Among the murders with known circumstances, an estimated 4,807 involved rape or a sex offense.

Figure 28

Sex offending and murder

Since the latter half of the 1980's, the percentage of all murders with known circumstances in which rape or other sex offenses have been identified by investigators as the principal circumstance underlying the murder has been declining from about 2% of murders to less than 1%.

Data on murder and murder victims and circumstances are obtained from the annual Supplemental Homicide Reporting (SHR) program of the FBI.

In the SHR, local law enforcement agencies report monthly a wide variety of information on each reported criminal homicide, differentiating murders and nonnegligent manslaughters from negligent manslaughters. Included are incident-based data on —
- the number of victims and offenders
- age, race, sex, and ethnic origin for victims and offenders
- type of weapon used
- victim-offender relationship
- a narrative statement about the circumstances of the homicide.

The narrative statements of circumstances are classified into 32 categories, including rape and other sex offenses. *Other sex offenses* includes sexual assaults such as statutory rape, sodomy, and incest and attempts to commit these crimes. Excluded from both of these categories of circumstances are commercial sex offenses such as prostitution or commercial vice.

● Between 1976 and 1994 there were an estimated 405,089 murders in the United States. Of these, the circumstances surrounding the murder are known in 317,925, or 78.5%. Among the cases with known circumstances, an estimated 4,807, or 1.5%,

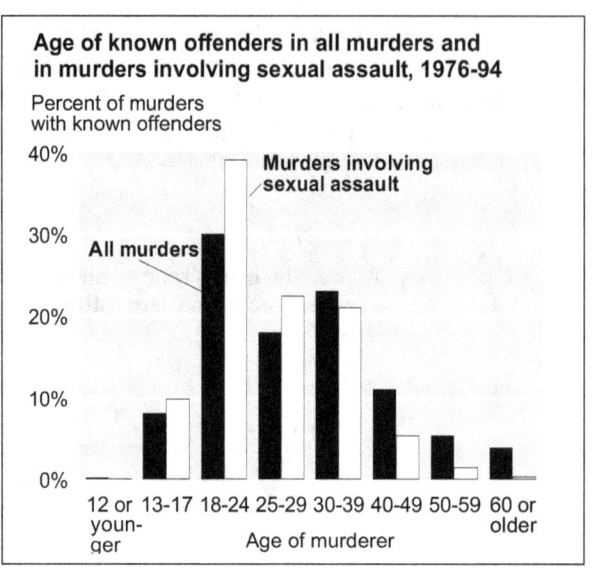

Age of known offenders in all murders and in murders involving sexual assault, 1976-94

Figure 29

were classified as involving rape or another sex offense.[3]

● In 1986 sexual assault murders accounted for 1.8% of murders with known circumstances; in 1994, an estimated 0.7% of murders involved sexual assault, the lowest percentage in the 19 years for which SHR data are available (figure 28).

● Known offenders in sexual assault murders are more likely to have been male than is true for murders in general (table 5). Sexual assault murders are also more likely than all murders to involve a white offender (58% versus 48%).

● Offenders in sexual assault murders are on average about 5 years younger than all murderers. More than 60% of sexual assault murderers, but less than 50% of all murderers, are between ages 18 and 29 (figure 29).

---

[3]Murders classified as involving rape or other sex offenses will be referred to as *sexual assault murders.*

Table 5. Characteristics of known offenders in murders involving sexual assault, 1976-94

| Offender characteristic | Murders | |
	All	Sexual assault
Sex		
Male	86.6%	95.0%
Female	13.4	5.0
Race		
White	47.8%	58.0%
Black	50.3	39.9
Other	1.9	2.1
Age		
12 or younger	.2%	.1%
13 to 17	8.1	9.9
18 to 24	30.1	39.1
25 to 29	18.0	22.5
30 to 39	23.1	21.1
40 to 49	11.1	5.4
50 to 59	5.4	1.5
60 or older	3.9	.4
Average	31 yrs	26 yrs

At age 60 or older, murderers in the aggregate are 10 times as likely to be found in this age group as those classified as sexual assault murderers. Youth under age 18 have accounted for about 10% of the sexual assault murders that have taken place since 1976.

• Sexual assault murder victims differ markedly from other murder victims. Compared to all murder victims, those who died as a consequence of a sexual assault were substantially more likely to be female and white. Sexual assault murder victims were both younger and older than the aggregate of all murder victims. More than 25% of sexual assault murder victims were under age 18, compared to about 15% of all murder victims. In addition, nearly 1 in 7 sexual assault murder victims were 60 or older, compared to 1 in 14 murder victims. Among victims, those age 13 to 17 (3.3% of whom died from a sexual assault murder) and those age 60 or older (2.6% died from a sexual assault murder) reflected the highest percentages killed under these circumstances (figure 30).

| | Murders | |
Victim characteristic	All	Sexual assault
Sex of victim		
Male	76.4%	18.0%
Female	23.6	82.0
Race of victim		
White	51.7%	68.4%
Black	46.3	28.9
Other	2.0	2.7
Age of victim		
12 or younger	10.1%	14.8%
13 to 17	4.6	9.7
18 to 24	21.3	21.7
25 to 29	15.7	12.3
30 to 39	22.0	14.2
40 to 49	11.7	8.3
50 to 59	6.9	5.3
60 or older	7.7	13.7
Average age	32 yrs	32 yrs

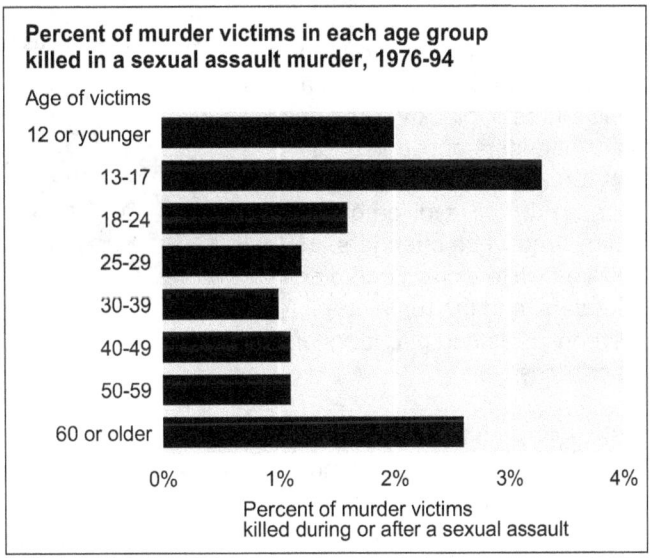

Percent of murder victims in each age group killed in a sexual assault murder, 1976-94

Age of victims

Percent of murder victims killed during or after a sexual assault

Figure 30

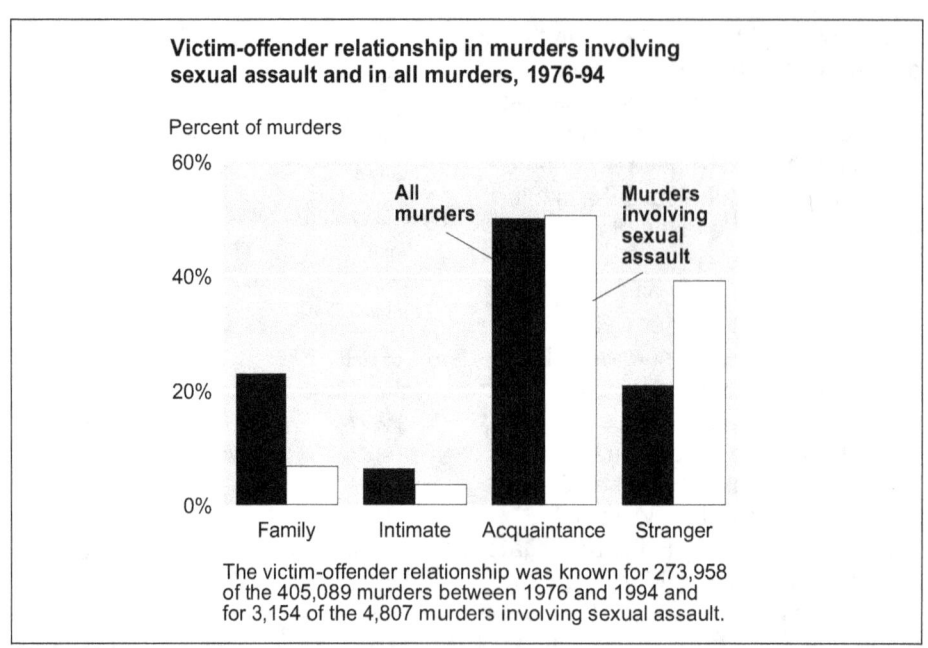

Victim-offender relationship in murders involving sexual assault and in all murders, 1976-94

Percent of murders

The victim-offender relationship was known for 273,958 of the 405,089 murders between 1976 and 1994 and for 3,154 of the 4,807 murders involving sexual assault.

Figure 31

• About 8 out of 10 sexual assault murders were intraracial. White victims and white offenders accounted for 55% of sexual assault murders, black victims and black offenders accounted for 24% of all murders involving sexual assault, 2% involved black victims and white offenders, 15% involved white victims and black offenders, and the remainder involved victims and offenders of other races.

• Sexual assault murders were about twice as likely as all murders (39.2% versus 20.9%) to involve victims and offenders who were strangers (figure 31). Sexual assault murders and all murders were equally likely to have involved acquaintances, but family murders were far less likely to have involved sexual assault.

Weapon or method used in murders involving sexual assault, 1976-94

Figure 32

• The most commonly used weapon in sexual assault murders was a knife (figure 32). About 2.2% of murders in which a knife was used involved sexual assault. Less than 0.4% of firearm murders involved sexual assault.

Glossary for U.S. statistical series: Defining sex offenses

As noted throughout the report, the statistical series differ in the types of offenses covered. The following series and their definitions of covered sex offenses are included:

National Crime Victimization Survey (NCVS)

Rape is defined as forced sexual intercourse in which the victim may be either male or female and the offender may be of a different sex or the same sex as the victim. Victims must be at least 12 years old; victims less than age 12 are excluded from all estimates. Includes attempts and threats to commit rape.

Sexual assault includes a wide range of victimizations involving attacks in which unwanted sexual contact occurs between the victim and offender. Includes threats and attempts to commit sexual assault.

Uniform Crime Reports (UCR) and Supplementary Homicide Reports (SHR)

Forcible rape is the carnal knowledge of a female forcibly and against her will. Assaults or attempts to commit rape by force or threat of force are also included; however, statutory rape (without force) and other sex offenses are excluded. Forcible rape is included as a Part I offense.

Sex offenses are limited to arrests only and exclude forcible rape, prostitution, and commercial vice; no data on sex offenses are included in the enumeration of Part I offenses. Sex offenses include sodomy, statutory rape, and offenses against chastity, decency, morals, and the like. Includes attempts.

National Incident-Based Reporting System (NIBRS)

Forcible rape is the carnal knowledge of a person forcibly and/or against that person's will; or not forcibly or against the person's will where the victim is incapable of giving consent because of his/her youth or because of his/her temporary or permanent mental or physical incapacity. This offense includes both male and female victims and threats and attempts.

Statutory rape is the carnal knowledge of a person without force or the threat of force when that person is below the statutory age of consent. The ability of the victim to give consent is a determination by the law enforcement agency.

Forcible sodomy is oral or anal sexual intercourse with another person, forcibly and/or against that person's will; or not forcibly or against that person's will where the victim is incapable of giving consent because of his/her youth or because of his/her temporary or permanent mental or physical incapacity.

Sexual assault with an object is a crime in which the offender uses an instrument or object to unlawfully penetrate the genital or anal opening of the body of another person, forcibly and/or against that person's will. The same characteristics apply in this offense, as in forcible rape and sodomy, regarding the ability of the victim to give consent.

Forcible fondling is the touching of the private body parts of another person for the purpose of sexual gratification, forcibly and/or against that person's will. The same limitations apply with respect to consent that are described for forcible rape and sodomy. Forcible fondling also includes indecent liberties and child molesting.

Incest is nonforcible sexual intercourse between persons who are related to each other within the degrees wherein marriage is prohibited by law.

National Pretrial Reporting Program (NPRP)

Rape includes forcible intercourse, sodomy, or penetration with a foreign object. Does not include statutory rape or nonforcible acts with a minor or someone unable to give legal consent, nonviolent sexual offenses, or commercialized sex offenses. Includes attempts.

National Judicial Reporting Program (NJRP)

Rape is forcible intercourse (vaginal, anal, or oral) with a female or male. Includes forcible sodomy or penetration with a foreign object. Does not include statutory rape or any other nonforcible sexual acts with a minor or with someone unable to give legal consent. Includes attempts.

Survey of Inmates in State Correctional Facilities (SISCF) and National Corrections Reporting Program (NCRP)

Forcible rape is forcible intercourse with a male or female. Includes attempts and conspiracies to commit rape.

Statutory rape is the carnal knowledge of a child without force. Includes attempts.

Lewd acts with children includes fondling, indecent liberties, immoral practices, molestation, and other indecent behaviors with children. Includes attempts.

Forcible sodomy includes deviate sexual intercourse, buggery, and oral or anal intercourse by force. Includes attempts.

Other sexual assault includes gross sexual imposition, sexual abuse, aggravated sexual abuse, and other acts such as fondling, molestation, or indecent liberties where the victim is not a child. Includes attempts.

Summary of definitional elements of rape and other sex offenses as used in U.S. Department of Justice statistical series

Statistical series	Victims		Includes		
	Age	Sex	Attempts?	Forcible rape?	Other sexual assault?
NCVS	Excludes under 12	Both	Yes	Yes	Yes, attacks involving un-wanted sexual contact.
UCR	All	Females only for rape	Yes	Yes	Limited to arrests only. Includes statutory rape and offenses against chastity, common decency, and morals.
NIBRS	All	Both	Yes	Yes	Yes, includes sodomy, fond-ling, incest, statutory rape, and sexual assault with an object.
NPRP	No victim data	No victim data	Yes	Yes	No.
NJRP	No victim data	No victim data	Yes	Yes	No.
SISCF	All	Both	Yes	Yes	Yes, includes forcible sod-omy, statutory rape, and lewd acts with children.
NCRP	Limited to of-fenses against children	No victim data	Yes	Yes	Yes, includes forc ble sod-omy, statutory rape, and lewd acts with children.
SHR	All	Both	Yes, but excludes attempted murder	Yes	Yes, includes statutory rape, sodomy, and incest.

Data points and sources for the graphical figures

Cover figure. About 234,000 convicted sex offenders are under the care, custody, or control of corrections agencies on an average day. Nearly 60% are under conditional supervision in the community.

Total	233,636
Probation	106,710
Local jails	10,345
State and Federal prisons	88,975
Parole	27,606

Source: BJS, National Crime Victimization Survey.

Figure 1, page 2. Estimated number of rape/sexual assault victimizations among residents age 12 or older and the number reported to law enforcement authorities, 1993-95

Year	Number of victimizations	Reported to law enforcement
1993	485,000	140,000
1994	433,000	137,000
1995	355,000	113,000

Source: BJS, National Crime Victimization Survey.

Figure 3, page 3. Victim's reports of where rapes and sexual assaults took place, 1993

	Percent of rape/sexual assault victimizations
At victim's home	37.4%
At friend's, neighbor's, or relative's home	19.2
On street away from home	10.0
Parking lot/garage	7.3
All other locations	26.1

Source: BJS, National Crime Victimization Survey.

Figure 7, page 6. Rate of forcible rape recorded by law enforcement agencies, 1976-95

Year	Number of forcible rapes of female victims per 100,000 females in the population
1976	52
1977	57
1978	60
1979	67
1980	71
1981	69
1982	65
1983	66
1984	69
1985	71
1986	73
1987	73
1988	73
1989	75
1990	80
1991	83
1992	84
1993	79
1994	77
1995	72

Source: FBI, Uniform Crime Reports, 1995.

Figure 8, page 8. Estimated number of arrests for forcible rape and other sex offenses, 1980-95

Year	Forcible rape	Other sex offenses	Total U.S. population
1980	31,380	67,400	227,726,463
1981	31,710	72,000	229,966,237
1982	33,600	78,800	232,187,835
1983	34,080	87,000	234,307,207
1984	36,700	97,800	236,348,292
1985	36,970	100,600	238,466,283
1986	37,140	100,600	240,650,755
1987	36,310	100,100	242,803,533
1988	38,310	106,300	245,021,414
1989	39,110	104,800	247,341,697
1990	39,160	107,600	249,912,527
1991	40,120	108,000	252,649,535
1992	39,100	108,400	255,418,704
1993	38,420	104,100	250,137,251
1994	36,610	100,700	260,659,690
1995	34,650	94,500	263,033,968

Source: FBI, Uniform Crime Reports, 1995.

Figure 9, page 9. Number of arrests per 100,000 for forcible rape and other sex offenses, by region 1995

Region	Forcible rape	Other sex offenses
U.S. total	13.5	36.8
Northeast	13.0	32.8
Midwest	15.7	37.3
South	14.6	32.0
West	10.7	46.6

Source: FBI, Uniform Crime Reports, 1995.

Figure 10, page 9. Number of arrests per 100,000 population for forcible rape and other sex offenses, by size of jurisdiction, 1995

Jurisdiction	Forcible rape	Other sex offenses
U.S. total	13.5	36.8
250,000 or more	22.0	58.0
249,999 - 100,000	15.8	40.9
99,999 - 50,000	12.0	35.0
49,999 - 25,000	9.9	29.3
24,999 - 10,000	10.6	26.3
9,999 or fewer	10.5	30.0
Suburban counties	10.5	29.8
Rural counties	11.4	30.6

Source: FBI, Uniform Crime Reports, 1995.

Figure 11, page 10. Age of persons arrested for forcible rape and for other sex offenses, 1995

Age of arrestees	Forcible rape	Other sex offenses
Less than 18	15.7%	16.9%
18-19	8.5	5.6
20-24	17.3	12.9
25-29	15.4	12.9
30-34	15.1	14.7
35-39	12.0	12.6
40-44	6.9	8.8
45-49	4.0	5.7
50-54	2.2	3.6
55-59	1.2	2.3
60 or older	1.7	3.7

Source: FBI, Uniform Crime Reports, 1995.

Figure 15, page 16. Number of offenders serving a sentence under supervision in the community per offender incarcerated in a prison or jail

Type of offense	Number of offenders
All offenses	2.8
DWI/DUI	11.9
Fraud	6.3
Public-order offenses	5.7
Larceny	5.3
Property offenses	3.6
Assault	3.2
Drug possession	3.0
Weapons offenses	2.9
Drug offenses	2.6
Burglary	2.1
Drug trafficking	2.1
Motor vehicle theft	1.8
Violent offenses	1.4
Sexual assault	1.4
Robbery	0.9
Homicide	0.4

Sources: BJS, corrections statistical series.

Figure 16, page 17. Estimated number of rape and sexual assault offenders in State correctional institutions, 1980-94

Year	Rape	Other sexual assault
1980	13,200	7,300
1981	15,000	9,400
1982	16,500	11,400
1983	17,000	12,000
1984	18,400	14,200
1985	19,400	20,300
1986	19,800	25,500
1987	21,000	29,700
1988	22,100	32,500
1989	22,600	35,400
1990	24,500	39,100
1991	25,500	43,000
1992	29,500	46,400
1993	32,600	48,800
1994	33,800	54,300

Source: BJS, *Correctional Populations in the United States, 1993* (NCJ-156241).

Figure 17, page 18. Average annual percent change in the number of State prisoners, by type of offense, 1980-94

	Average annual percent change, 1980-94
All offenses	7.6%
Violent offenses	6.7
Murder	7.6
Robbery	4.0
Assault	9.2
Forc ble rape	6.9
Other sexual assault	15.4
Property offenses	6.3%
Drug offenses	18.4%

Source: BJS, *Correctional Populations in the United States, 1993* (NCJ-156241).

Figure 19, page 19. Average sentence received for rape and sexual assault, State prison admissions, 1985-93

Year	Rape	Other sexual assault
1985	147	105
1986	152	105
1987	157	105
1988	156	97
1989	148	98
1990	149	97
1991	140	99
1992	144	99
1993	141	108

Source: BJS, National Corrections Reporting Program.

Figure 20, page 20. Average prison sentence received for rape and time served in State prison prior to first release, 1985-93

Year	Average sentence in months	Average time served in months
1985	105	41
1986	121	45
1987	122	47
1988	117	45
1989	115	51
1990	123	55
1991	117	56
1992	117	59
1993	117	57

Source: BJS, National Corrections Reporting Program.

Figure 21, page 20. Average prison sentence and time served for sexual assault (excluding rape), State prison releases, 1985-93

Year	Average sentence in months	Average time served in months
1985	77	26
1986	77	27
1987	77	29
1988	75	27
1989	76	29
1990	77	30
1991	76	31
1992	75	30
1993	80	33

Source: BJS, National Corrections Reporting Program.

Figure 24, page 23. State inmates reporting physical or sexual abuse occurring before prison and inmates reporting abuse as children, by selected offenses

Current offense	Physically/ sexually abused	Abused as children
All inmates	13.7%	11.8%
Murder	17.3	14.2
Rape	20.8	19.3
Other sexual assault	34.9	34.0
Robbery	10.8	9.4
Assault	14.0	11.7
Burglary	12.6	11.0
Larceny	11.3	8.9

Source: BJS, 1991 Survey of Inmates in State Correctional Facilities.

Figure 22, page 21. State prison inmates serving time for rape or sexual assault, by age at arrest

Age at arrest	Percent of inmates
Younger than 18	5.9%
18-24	13.9
25-29	16.3
30-34	21.9
35-39	28.1
40-44	31.8
45-49	34.8
50-54	45.4
55-59	50.6
60 or older	36.2

Source: BJS, 1991 Survey of Inmates in State Correctional Facilities.

Figure 28, page 27. Murders involving rape or other sexual assault, as a percentage of murders with known circumstances, 1976-94

Year	Percent of murders involving rape or other sexual assault
1976	1.9%
1977	1.9
1978	1.5
1979	1.8
1980	1.6
1981	1.6
1982	1.6
1983	1.8
1984	1.8
1985	1.8
1986	1.8
1987	1.7
1988	1.5
1989	1.3
1990	1.3
1991	1.1
1992	1.1
1993	.8
1994	.7

Source: FBI, Supplementary Homicide Reports.

Figure 29, page 28. Age of known offenders in all murders and in murders involving sexual assault, 1976-94

Age at arrest	All murders	Murders involving sexual assault
12 or younger	.2%	.1%
13-17	8.1	9.9
18-24	30.1	39.1
25-29	18.0	22.5
30-39	23.1	21.1
40-49	11.1	5.4
50-59	5.4	1.5
60 or older	3.9	.4

Source: FBI, Supplementary Homicide Reports.

Figure 30, page 29. Percent of murder victims in each age group killed in a sexual assault murder, 1976-94

Age of victims	Percent of murder victims
12 or younger	2.0%
13-17	3.3
18-24	1.6
25-29	1.2
30-39	1.0
40-49	1.1
50-59	1.1
60 or older	2.6

Source: FBI, Supplementary Homicide Reports.

Figure 31, page 30. Victim-offender relationship in murders involving sexual assault and in all murders, 1976-94

	Percent of murders	
	All murders	Murders involving sexual assault
Family	22.9%	6.7%
Intimate	6.3	3.5
Acquaintance	50.0	50.6
Stranger	20.9	39.2

Source: FBI, Supplementary Homicide Reports.

Basic sources

The following publications and other materials about criminal justice issues can be found by requesting them from the BJS Clearinghouse, Box 179, Annapolis Junction, MD 20701-0179, or by calling 1-800-732-3277.

Most reports are also available at the BJS World Wide Web site —
   http://www.ojp.usdoj.gov/bjs/

National Crime Victimization Survey

Criminal Victimization in the United States, 1993, BJS, May 1996, NCJ-151657.

National Prisoner Statistics and Probation and Parole Data Surveys and Survey of Inmates in State Correctional Facilities

Child Victimizers: Violent Offenders and Their Victims, BJS, March 1996, NCJ-161132.

BJS, *Correctional Populations in the United States,* selected years.

BJS, *National Corrections Reporting Program,* selected years.

Prisoners and Jail Inmates, 1995, BJS, August 1996, NCJ-161132.

Prisoners in 1994, BJS, August 1995, NCJ-151654.

National Judicial Reporting Program

State Court Sentencing of Convicted Felons, 1992, BJS, May 1996, NCJ-152696.

National Pretrial Reporting Program (State Court Processing Statistics)

Felony Defendants in Large Urban Counties, 1992, BJS, July 1995, NCJ-148826.

Offender-Based Tracking Survey

Tracking Offenders, 1990, BJS, June 1994, NCJ-148200.

National Incident-Based Reporting System

Using NIBRS Data to Analyze Violent Crime, BJS, October 1993, NCJ-144785.

Supplementary Homicide Reports

FBI, National Archive of Criminal Justice Data, accessible through —
   http://www.icpsr.umich.edu/NACJD/
      home.html
   search for data (DA): 6754

Uniform Crime Reports

FBI, *Crime in the United States,* selected years.